also by Ken Hom

Ken Hom's Quick Wok

The fastest food in the East

photographs by jeremy hopley

headline

Photographs © 2001 Jeremy Hopley

First published in 2001
by HEADLINE BOOK PUBLISHING

First published in paperback in 2003
by HEADLINE BOOK PUBLISHING

10 9 8 7 6 5 4 3 2 1

ISBN 0 7472 7600 5

Art direction and design by Fiona Knowles, Pike Design
Home economy and food styling by Meg Jansz
Styling by Wei Tang

Printed and bound in France by Imprimerie Pollina s.a. - n° L87870

HEADLINE BOOK PUBLISHING
A division of Hodder Headline
338 Euston Road
London NW1 3BH

www.headline.co.uk
www.hodderheadline.com

A full range of **Ken Hom Woks and Utensils** is sold by William Levene Ltd. A list of stockists in the UK and overseas is available from Customer Services on 020 8868 4355.

contents

Dedication

To my uncle, Paul Lee, who not only taught me
how to cook but how to work as well

Acknowledgements

It takes many people to put a book together. I have perhaps
the easiest task, that of writing; however, I would be lost
without Heather Holden-Brown's inspiration and guidance, and
Gordon Wing's meticulous testing of each recipe. The skilful
eye of copy editor Celia Levett has helped to make the recipes
more coherent and lucid, and those at Headline and the design
company have combined with photographer Jeremy Hopley
and his team to create a beautiful book that is both modern
and useful. So thanks to: Fiona Knowles, Liz Allen, Lorraine
Jerram, Kate Truman, Meg Jansz and Wei Tang.

introduction

Cooking quickly comes naturally with the wok. The hot temperatures and ease of use make using the wok ideal for modern life. As time becomes more valuable, elaborate meals with many courses are rarer or are relegated to long weekends.

However, good food is essential for health and well-being. No ready-cooked meal can take the place of fresh food cooked with love, nor can it replace the comforting smell of fresh vegetables simply stir-fried with garlic or ginger. At the end of the day, it comes down to quality of life versus compromise.

Quick cooking does not imply bad cooking. It is a matter of organisation, the right recipes and experience. That is what this book is all about: using the wok in a sensible and easy manner.

Once your shopping and preparation are done, the cooking in most cases is literally a matter of minutes. Some recipes may require marinating to infuse the food with the necessary flavour for a delicious meal.

Certain recipes have a stage up to which they can be prepared in advance. This is indicated by the symbol **P**, and additional information is given where required.

It all adds up to great, tasty food without compromise. With my busy lifestyle, I find that using the wok is the perfect answer to today's fast-pace demands. Use these quick recipes in good health!

MEASURES

All spoon measurements are level. A teaspoon is 5ml and a tablespoon 15ml. Egg sizes are medium throughout. The metric and imperial equivalents in the recipes have been rounded up or down as necessary. In a few recipes, they have been slightly modified. Always use one set of measurements or the other in a recipe; don't mix them.

EQUIPMENT

WOKS

The most versatile piece of cooking equipment ever invented, the wok may be used for stir-frying, blanching, deep-frying and steaming foods. Its shape, with deep sides and either a tapered or a slightly flattened but still round bottom, allows for fuel-efficient, quick, even heating and cooking.

There are two basic wok types: the traditional Cantonese version, with short rounded handles on either side of the edge or lip of the wok; and the pau or Peking wok, which has one long handle from 30 to 35cm (12 to 14 in) long. The long-handled wok keeps you more safely distanced from hot oils or water.

You should be aware that the round-bottomed wok may only be used on a gas hob. Woks are now available with flatter bottoms, designed especially for electric hobs. Although this shape really defeats the purpose of the traditional design, which is to concentrate intense heat at the centre, it does have the advantage over ordinary frying pans in that it has deeper sides.

All the recipes in this book are designed to be cooked in a wok. However, if you don't have one, you can use either a large frying pan for stir-frying recipes, or a large deep saucepan for steaming recipes.

Choosing a wok

Choose a large wok – preferably about 30 to 35cm (12 to 14 in) in diameter, with deep sides. It is easier, and safer, to cook a small batch of food in a large wok than a large quantity in a small one.

You should be aware that some modernised woks are too shallow or too flat-bottomed and thus no better than an ordinary frying pan. A heavier wok, preferably made of carbon steel, is superior to the lighter stainless-steel or aluminium type, which cannot take very high heat and tends to blacken and scorch the food. Good, non-stick, carbon-steel woks that maintain the heat without sticking are now on the market. However, these woks need special care to prevent scratching. In recent years, non-stick technology has improved vastly, so that they can now be safely recommended. They are especially useful when cooking foods that have a high acid level, such as lemons. You will see that a non-stick wok is recommended for some of the recipes in this book. Ordinary uncoated carbon steel or iron may react with some foods, turning them grey. This is not harmful, but is unappealing.

Seasoning a wok

All woks (except non-stick ones) need to be seasoned. Many also need to be scrubbed first to remove the machine oil applied to the surface by the manufacturer to protect it in transit. This is the only time you will ever scrub your wok – unless you let it rust up.

Scrub it with a cream cleanser and water to remove as much of the machine oil as possible. Then dry it and put it on the hob on a low heat. Add 2 tablespoons of cooking oil and, using kitchen paper, rub it over the inside of the wok until the entire surface is lightly coated with oil. Heat the wok slowly for about 10–15 minutes and then wipe it thoroughly with more kitchen paper. The paper will become blackened from the machine oil. Repeat this process of coating, heating and wiping until the kitchen paper comes clean. Your wok will darken and become seasoned with use, which is a good sign.

Cleaning a wok

Once your wok has been seasoned, it should never be scrubbed with soap and water. Plain clean water is all that is needed. The wok should be thoroughly dried after each use. Putting the cleaned wok over low heat for a minute or two

should do the trick. If by any chance it does rust a bit, then it must be scrubbed with a cream cleanser and re-seasoned.

WOK ACCESSORIES

Wok stand

This is a metal ring or frame designed to keep a conventionally shaped wok (one with a completely rounded bottom) steady on the hob; it is an essential aid if you want to use your wok for steaming, deep-frying or braising.

Stands come in two designs. One is a solid metal ring with about six ventilation holes. The other is like a circular thin wire frame. If you have a gas cooker, use only the latter type; the more solid design does not allow for sufficient ventilation and may lead to a build-up of gas which could put the flame out completely.

Wok lid

This light domed cover, usually made from aluminium, is used for steaming. The lid normally comes with the wok, but if not, it may be purchased at a Chinese or Asian grocer; alternatively, you can use any domed pot lid that fits snugly.

Spatula

A long-handled metal spatula shaped rather like a small shovel is ideal for scooping and tossing food in a wok. Alternatively, any good long-handled spoon can be used.

Rack

When steaming food in your wok, you will need a wooden or metal rack or trivet to keep the food to be cooked above water level. Wok sets usually include a rack, but if not, Asian and Chinese grocers sell them separately. Department stores and hardware shops also sell wooden and metal stands that serve the same purpose.

Bamboo brush

This bundle of stiff, split bamboo is used for cleaning a wok without scrubbing away the seasoned surface. It is an attractive, inexpensive implement but not essential. A soft washing-up brush will do just as well.

DEEP-FAT FRYER

This is very useful, and you may find it is safer and easier to use for deep-frying than a wok. The quantities of oil given in the recipes are based on the amount required for deep-frying in a wok. If you are using a deep-fat fryer instead, you will need about double the amount, but never fill it more than half full with oil.

CLEAVER

The cleaver is an all-purpose cutting instrument. Once you gain facility with a cleaver, you will see how it can be used on all types of food to slice, dice, chop, fillet, shred, crush or whatever. Most Asian chefs rely upon three different sizes of cleaver – light, medium and heavy – to be used as appropriate. Of course, you may use your own familiar kitchen knives, but if you decide to invest in a cleaver, choose a good-quality stainless-steel model and keep it sharpened.

CHOPPING BOARD

One decided improvement over the traditional implements of Chinese cooking is the modern chopping board made of hardwood or white acrylic. Both types are easy to clean, resist bacterial accumulation and last a much longer time.

Chinese cookery entails much chopping, slicing and dicing, so it is essential to have a dependable, large and steady chopping board. For reasons of hygiene, never place cooked meat on a board on which raw meat or poultry has been prepared. For raw meat, always use a separate board and clean it thoroughly after each use.

INGREDIENTS

BAMBOO SHOOTS

Bamboo shoots generally fall into two broad categories: spring shoots and winter shoots, the winter being smaller and more tender than the spring ones, which tend to be quite large. Fresh bamboo shoots are sweet and crunchy with an unforgettable, distinctive taste. They are too fragile to export, and I have only rarely seen them in Chinese markets in the West. We have to be satisfied with the tinned varieties, which are at least more reasonably priced. Tinned bamboo shoots tend to be pale yellow with a crunchy texture and, in some cases, a slightly sweet flavour. They come peeled and either whole or thickly sliced. Buy whole bamboo shoots, rather than sliced. They tend to hold their flavour better. In some Chinese markets, bamboo shoots preserved in brine are available and these tend to have much more flavour than the tinned variety.

Many of the brands from China are tasty, especially the winter shoots; the Ma Ling brand is recommended. I have generally found brands from Taiwan to be relatively bland. Purchase the preserved brine variety if they are available in open bins in the refrigerated section of Chinese grocers.

Rinse tinned bamboo shoots thoroughly and blanch them for 2 minutes in boiling water before use. Transfer any remaining shoots to a jar, cover them with fresh water and refrigerate. If the water is changed daily, they will keep for 2 to 3 days.

BASIL

Although coriander is used extensively in cooking throughout Asia, basil is probably only used in Vietnam and Thailand. It is from my many visits to Thailand that I have acquired a love for the use of basil. It adds a refreshing and tart aniseed note to many dishes, yet it is subtle.

BEANCURD

Beancurd is also known by its Chinese name, doufu, or in Japanese, tofu. It is highly nutritious, rich in protein and low in calories. It has a distinctive texture but a bland taste, which makes it a congenial companion to other foods and spices. It is made from yellow soya beans, which are soaked, ground, mixed with water and then cooked briefly before being solidified.

In the UK it is usually sold in two fresh forms: 'soft', which is a thick junket, and 'firm', which is in the form of solid cakes. It is also available in several dried forms and in a fermented version. The soft junket-like variety, sometimes called silken tofu, is used for soups, while the more solid firm type is used for stir-frying, braising and poaching.

Beancurd can be found in some health-food shops and, of course, in Chinese supermarkets and grocers, usually in the refrigerated section. It is often sold in vacuum-packed plastic and should be stored in the refrigerator for up to a week. Once opened, it should be used within two or three days. Alternatively, it may be packed in water in plastic containers. It can be kept in this state in the refrigerator for up to five days, provided the water is changed daily.

Also available is pressed and seasoned beancurd, which is seasoned, usually with soy sauce, and pressed until most of the water has been extracted. It has a dry, chewy texture. This makes the beancurd firm and compact. It can also be smoked for additional flavour. Found in many health-food shops, it is a great substitute for meat.

To use solid beancurd, cut the amount required into cubes or shreds using a sharp knife. Do this with care, as it is delicate and it may break apart. It also needs to be cooked carefully, as too much stirring can cause it to crumble. Fortunately, it needs little cooking, which makes it a perfect stir-fry ingredient.

Cut into small pieces, beancurd can be stir-fried with meat or vegetables; when cut into larger pieces it can be simmered with soy sauce, star anise and sugar, when it acquires a smooth, resilient texture that is quite unusual. For vegetarian dishes, simply brush beancurd cakes with oil and grill them, or add them instead of meat to vegetables for a tasty main course.

BEANSPROUTS

These are the sprouts of the green mung bean: they contribute a crisp texture and their own barely discernible flavour to any dish. Fresh beansprouts are readily available. Always use fresh sprouts, and never the soggy tinned version. They will keep for several days when loosely wrapped in kitchen paper inside a plastic bag in the vegetable crisper of a refrigerator.

The larger, yellow soya beansprouts may be substituted, but avoid alfalfa, wheat and rye sprouts: they just don't do the job.

BITTER MELON

Bitter melon has a bumpy, dark to pale green skin, and has a slightly bitter quinine flavour that has a cooling effect in the mouth. Not surprisingly, it was originally prized for its supposed medicinal qualities: something so bitter had to be good medicine. In some parts of China, it is thought to purify the blood and cool the digestive system, and it is often dried for medicinal use. The greener the melon, the more bitter its taste, and most cooks wisely look for the milder yellow-green varieties.

This tropical fruit's fibrous seed core is usually cut away, leaving a thin ring of flesh. It is stir-fried, steamed, quickly braised or used in soups. A popular recipe, which reduces its bitterness, is to stuff it with seasoned pork and steam it. It is often paired with strong pungent ingredients, such as black beans, garlic or chilli, whose flavours tone down the melon's bitterness. Store it in the bottom of the refrigerator in a loose plastic or paper bag. It will keep there for about 3 to 5 days, depending on the condition in which it was bought.

To use, cut in half, deseed and discard the interior membrane. Then, to reduce its bitter taste, either blanch or salt it, according to the instructions in the recipe.

BLACK BEANS

These small black soya beans, also known as salted black beans, are preserved through fermentation with salt and spices. They have a distinctive, slightly salty taste and a rich pleasant smell, and make a tasty seasoning, especially when used in conjunction with garlic or fresh ginger.

They are inexpensive and can be obtained from Chinese or Asian grocers, usually in tins labelled 'Black Beans in Salted Sauce', but you may also find them packed in plastic bags.

You can rinse them before use, although this is optional. I prefer to chop them slightly, as this releases their pungent flavour. Transfer any unused beans and liquid to a sealed jar; the beans will keep indefinitely if stored in the refrigerator.

CHILLIES

Chillies come in many colours, in hundreds of varieties and in different degrees of intensity ('hotness') but few are commercially available. Their 'heat' varies, depending on the seeds, how they are grown, the variety, the season and many other factors. You will need to experiment with different varieties to find the right degree of 'heat' to suit your taste.

Chillies are the seed pods of the capsicum plant and can be obtained fresh, dried or ground. Removing the seeds, the source of most of the chilli 'heat', reduces the heat intensity but still leaves much rich flavour.

Fresh chillies

These should look fresh and bright with no brown patches or black spots. Red chillies tend to be milder than green (because they sweeten as they ripen), and larger ones milder than small. Small red or green Thai chillies, for instance, are especially pungent and strong.

To prepare fresh chillies, first rinse them in cold water. Then, using a small sharp knife, slit them lengthways. For most uses, remove and discard the seeds. Rinse the chillies well under cold running water, and then prepare them according to the recipe's instructions. Wash your hands, knife and chopping board before preparing other foods, and be very careful not to touch your eyes until you have washed your hands thoroughly with soap and water.

Chilli powder

Chilli powder is made from dried red chillies and commonly some other spices and seasonings. It is pungent, aromatic and ranges from 'hot' to 'very hot'. You will be able to buy chilli powder in any supermarket. As with chillies in general, your own palate will determine the degree of 'hotness' that is acceptable to you. 'Use sparingly' are the watchwords for beginners.

Chilli bean sauce (see Sauces and Pastes, page 17)

Chilli oil

In the same way that chillies vary in strength and flavour, so do chilli oils. Thai and Malaysian versions are especially 'hot'; Taiwanese and Chinese versions are more subtle. You can purchase chilli oil from Thai markets. Such commercial products are quite acceptable, but I include this recipe because the home-made version is the best.

Remember that chilli oil is too dramatic to be used directly as the sole cooking oil; it is best used as part of a dipping sauce or as a condiment, or combined with other milder oils. I include pepper and black beans in this recipe for additional flavour because I also use it as a dipping sauce.

Once made, put the chilli oil in a tightly sealed glass jar and store in a cool dark place, where it will keep for months.

chilli oil/chilli dipping sauce

2 tablespoons chopped dried red chillies
1 tablespoon whole unroasted Sichuan peppercorns
2 tablespoons whole black beans
150ml (5 fl oz) groundnut (peanut) oil

Heat a wok over high heat until it is hot. Add the oil and the rest of the ingredients, turn the heat down to low and cook over a low heat for about 10 minutes. Allow to cool undisturbed and then pour into a jar. Let it stand for 2 days, and then strain the oil. It will keep indefinitely.

COCONUT MILK

Coconut milk is not only drunk as a popular cooling beverage in South-East Asia; it is also used extensively by cooks – in curries and stews, often combined with curry pastes for sauces, and as a key ingredient in desserts and candies.

The milk itself is the liquid wrung from the grated and pressed coconut meat which is then combined with water. It has some of the properties of cow's milk: for example, the 'cream' (fatty globules) rises to the top when the milk is left to stand; it must be stirred as it comes to the boil; and its fat is closer in chemical composition to butterfat than to vegetable fat.

In Thai markets, and more rarely in Chinese grocers, it may be possible to find freshly made coconut milk, especially in neighbourhoods where there is a large Thai or South-East Asian population. Fortunately, however, there are inexpensive tinned versions (usually in 14 fl oz or 15 fl oz cans – around 400ml), which can be found in supermarkets and specialist Thai food shops. Many of the available brands are high quality and quite acceptable, and I recommend them. Look in particular for those from Thailand or Malaysia.

Be sure to shake the tin well before opening.

CORIANDER (CHINESE PARSLEY, CILANTRO OR PAK CHEE)

Fresh coriander is one of the most popular herbs used in South-East Asian cookery. It looks like flat parsley but its pungent, musky, citrus-like flavour gives it a distinctive character that is unmistakable. Its feathery leaves are often used as a garnish, or they can be chopped and mixed into sauces and stuffings. Many Thai and Chinese grocers stock it, as do some greengrocers and, increasingly, local supermarkets.

When buying fresh coriander, look for deep green, fresh-looking leaves. Yellow and limp leaves indicate age and should be avoided. To store coriander, wash it in cold water, drain it thoroughly (use a salad spinner to spin the fresh coriander dry) and wrap it in kitchen paper. Store it in the vegetable compartment of your refrigerator where it should keep for several days.

Coriander, ground

Ground coriander, made from coriander seeds, has a fresh, lemon-like sweet flavour. Widely used in curry mixes, it can be purchased already ground. However, the best method is to toast whole coriander seeds in the oven and then finely grind them.

CURRY POWDER, MADRAS

Although Western-style curry powders are quite different from those used in Indian cuisine, there are many reliable commercial brands that are used by Asian cooks because their exotic flavours and subtle aromas can add so much to a dish. Remember: curry is a term that refers to a style of cookery and not to a single taste or degree of spiciness.

FIVE-SPICE POWDER

Five-spice powder is less commonly known as five-flavoured powder or five-fragrance spice powder, and it is becoming a staple in the spice section of many supermarkets. Thai or Chinese grocers always stock it.

This versatile spice is a mixture of star anise, Sichuan peppercorns, fennel, cloves and cinnamon. A good blend is pungent, fragrant, spicy and slightly sweet at the same time. The exotic fragrance it gives to a dish makes the search for it well worth the effort. It keeps indefinitely in a well-sealed jar.

GARLIC

This common, nutritious and very popular seasoning, a cousin of the onion, is used by Asian cooks in numerous ways: whole, finely chopped, crushed or pickled. It flavours curries, spicy sauces, soups and practically every dish on the menu.

Choose fresh garlic that is firm and preferably pinkish in colour. Store it in a cool, dry place, but not in the refrigerator where it can easily become mildewed or begin sprouting.

GINGER

Fresh root ginger is an indispensable ingredient in Asian cookery. Its pungent, spicy, fresh taste adds a subtle but distinctive flavour to soups, meats and vegetables. It is also an important seasoning for fish and seafood since it neutralises any fishy aromas.

Root ginger looks rather like a gnarled Jerusalem artichoke and pieces can range in length from 7.5cm (3 in) to 15cm (6 in). It has pale brown, dry skin, which is usually peeled away before use. Select fresh ginger that is firm with no signs of shrivelling. It will keep in the refrigerator, well wrapped in cling film, for up to two weeks.

Fresh ginger can now be bought at most Asian markets as well as at many greengrocers and supermarkets. Dried powdered ginger has a quite different flavour and should be used only as a last resort.

Ginger juice

Ginger juice is made from fresh ginger and is used in marinades to give a subtle taste of ginger without the bite of fresh chopped pieces. To prepare ginger juice, cut unpeeled fresh ginger into 2.5cm (1 in) chunks and drop into a running food processor. When the ginger is finely chopped, squeeze out the juice by hand through a cotton or linen teatowel.

Alternatively, mash some fresh ginger using a kitchen mallet or the flat of a cleaver or knife, until most of the fibres are exposed. Then simply squeeze out the juice by hand through a cotton or linen teatowel. A piece of ginger 7.5 x 2.5cm (3 x 1 in) long will yield about 1 tablespoon.

LEMONGRASS

The subtle lemony fragrance and flavour of this herb impart a very special cachet to delicate foods and make it a standard ingredient in some Asian dishes, particularly in Thailand, where it is also considered a medicinal agent, prescribed often for digestive disorders.

This South-East Asian original is available in fresh as well as dried form (although the dried form is not used for cooking, but as a herbal tea). Lemongrass is closely related to citronella grass, but latter has a stronger oil content and is more likely to be used commercially in perfumes and as a mosquito repellent. The two relatives should not be confused.

Fresh lemongrass is sold in stalks that can be 60cm (2 ft) long – it looks like a very long, thin spring onion. Most recipes use only the bottom few inches of the stem. It is a fibrous plant but this is no problem because what is wanted is its fragrance and taste. Whole lemongrass pieces are always removed from a dish before it is served.

Get the freshest possible lemongrass: this is usually found in Thai or other Asian markets. However, it is becoming increasingly available in many supermarkets. Lemongrass can be kept, loosely wrapped, in the bottom part of your refrigerator for up to one week. Please note that lemon is not a substitute for the unique flavours of lemongrass.

LIME

This small citrus green fruit is a native of southern Asia but is now a global favourite. It has a delicate, fresh, tart taste that is widely used in Asia to impart zest to food or as a base for sauces. Both the juice and the peel can add a unique taste dimension to many dishes. One average lime will yield approximately 2 tablespoons of juice and 1½ teaspoons of zest.

MIRIN (JAPANESE SWEET RICE WINE)

A heavy, sweet Japanese rice wine with a light syrup texture. It is used only in cooking, to add a mild sweetness to sauces or foods. It is especially delicious with grilled foods as once the alcohol is burned off, only the sweet essence of the Mirin remains. There is no substitute for this unique item. It can be found in many Chinese or Asian supermarkets or Japanese speciality food shops. One bottle will last quite a long time and is well worth the search.

MOOLI OR CHINESE WHITE RADISH

Like Western radishes, mooli is a pungent root with a peppery taste. It is long and parsnip-shaped and is usually cooked. It is generally available from supermarkets, or may be found in Asian grocers.

MUSHROOMS

Three types of mushrooms are used in these recipes: the familiar button, shiitake and Chinese dried mushrooms.

Chinese dried mushrooms

Dried mushrooms add a special flavour and texture to Asian dishes, and their rich, smoky aroma is much prized. They come in many varieties, either black or brown in colour. The very large ones with a lighter colour and a cracked surface are the best. These are usually also the most expensive, so use them with a light touch. Chinese dried mushrooms can be bought in boxes or plastic bags from Chinese and Asian grocers. Store them in an air-tight jar. To use Chinese dried mushrooms, soak them in a bowl of warm water for about 20 minutes or until they are soft and pliable. Squeeze out the excess water and cut off and discard the woody stems. Only the caps are used. The soaking water can be saved and used in soups and for cooking rice, to add extra flavour. Strain the liquid through a fine sieve to discard any sand or residue from the dried mushrooms.

Shiitake mushrooms

These mushrooms figure largely in Asian cooking. They are

dark brown in colour and have a pleasant, distinctive flavour. They are usually available in supermarkets, and from Asian grocers. Shiitake mushrooms are sold fresh.

NOODLES

Like rice, noodles provide the substance of nutritious, quick, sustaining meals, as well as the makings of light snacks. Both fresh and dried noodles are available from Chinese or Asian grocers, and may sometimes be found in supermarkets.

Three types of noodles are used in these recipes: beanthread, egg and dried rice.

Beanthread (transparent) noodles

These transparent noodles, also called cellophane noodles, are made from ground mung beans, not from a grain flour. They are available dried and are very fine and white. Easy to recognise in their neat plastic-wrapped bundles, they are stocked by Chinese markets and supermarkets. Beanthread noodles are never served on their own. Instead, they are added to soups or braised dishes or are deep-fried and used as a garnish.

They must be soaked in hot water for at least 5 minutes before use. As they are rather long, you might find it easier to cut them into shorter lengths after soaking. If you are frying them, they do not need soaking beforehand, but they do need to be separated. A good technique for doing this is to pull them apart inside a large paper bag, which stops them from flying all over the place.

Egg noodles

These are made from hard or soft wheat flour and water. Supermarkets and delicatessens usually stock both the dried and fresh variety. Flat noodles are usually used in soups, and rounded noodles are best for stir-frying or pan-frying. The fresh ones freeze nicely if they are well wrapped. Thaw them thoroughly before cooking. Noodles are very good blanched and served with main dishes instead of plain rice. I think fresh egg noodles are best for this.

To cook egg noodles

225g (8 oz) fresh or dried egg or wheat noodles
If you are using fresh noodles, immerse them in a pot of boiling water and cook them for 3–5 minutes or until done to your taste. If you are using dried noodles, either cook them according to the instructions on the package, or cook them in boiling water for 4–5 minutes. Drain and serve.

If you are cooking noodles ahead of time or before stir-frying them, toss the cooked and drained noodles in 2 teaspoons of sesame oil and put them into a bowl. Cover this with cling film and refrigerate. The cooked noodles will remain nicely usable for about 2 hours.

Rice noodles

These dried noodles are opaque white and come in a variety of shapes. Thin noodles are similar to Italian cappellini. Flat noodles are similar to Italian fettuccine. Both types can be made from eggs and rice flour, or just plain rice flour. They are both cooked in the same way.

Rice stick noodles, which are flat and about the length of a chopstick, are one of the most common. They can also vary in thickness. Use the type called for in each recipe.

Rice noodles are very easy to prepare. Simply soak them in hot water for 20 minutes until they are soft. Drain them in a colander or a sieve, and then they are ready to be used in soups or a stir-fry.

OILS

Oil is the most commonly used cooking medium in South-East Asia. My favourite is groundnut (peanut) oil. Animal fats, usually lard and chicken fat, are also used in some areas, but vegetable oils – peanut, soybean, safflower – are increasingly the choice of many Asian cooks.

Oil can sometimes be reused. Simply cool the oil after use and filter it through cheesecloth, muslin or a fine strainer into a jar. Cover it tightly and keep in a cool, dry place. If you keep it in the refrigerator, it will become cloudy, but it will clarify again when the oil returns to room temperature.

I find oils are best reused just once, which is healthier because constantly reused oils increase in saturated fat content.

Groundnut (peanut) oil

This is also known as arachide oil. I prefer to use this for wok cookery because it has a pleasant, unobtrusive taste. Although it has a higher saturated fat content than some other oils, its ability to be heated to a high temperature without burning makes it perfect for stir-frying and deep-frying. Most supermarkets stock it, but if you cannot find it, use corn oil instead.

Corn oil

Corn or maize oil is also quite suitable for wok cooking, as it has a high heating point. It is also rich in polyunsaturates and therefore one of the healthier oils. However, I find it rather bland, with a slightly disagreeable smell.

Other vegetable oils

Some of the cheaper vegetable oils available include soybean, safflower and sunflower. They are light in colour and taste, and can also be used for wok cooking, but they smoke and burn at lower temperatures than groundnut oil, so care must be taken when cooking with them.

Extra-virgin olive oil

Where this is stipulated, use the best-quality extra-virgin oil you can find. It is not the ideal oil for wok cookery, because its rich fruity taste is destroyed by high heat. However, nothing beats the taste of olive oil in salads and cold dishes, and it is the perfect complement to dishes with tomatoes.

In some of these recipes, you will find it combined with groundnut oil. This is not only an example of fusion cookery – where Eastern and Western ingredients are combined for a new and different taste – but is also done for a practical reason: the groundnut oil prevents the olive oil from burning, which would destroy all its delicious flavour.

Sesame oil

This thick, rich, golden-brown oil made from sesame seeds has a distinctive, nutty flavour and aroma. It is widely used in Asian cookery as a seasoning but is not normally used as a cooking oil because it heats rapidly and burns easily. Therefore, think of it more as a flavouring than as a cooking oil. It is often added at the last moment to finish a dish. Sold in bottles, it is available from Asian or Chinese grocers and many supermarkets.

PEPPER

Black pepper

Black pepper is an essential part of Asian marinades, pastes and condiments. The peppercorns are unripe berries from a vine of the *Piperaceae* family, which are picked, fermented and dried until they are hard and black. They are best when freshly ground.

White pepper

White peppercorns do not occur naturally; they are an artefact. They are made from the largest of the ripe peppercorn berries, which are suspended in running water for several days. The berries swell, making the removal of the outer skin easier; the pale inner seeds are then sun-dried, which turns them a pale beige colour. Hence, white peppercorns. Again, they are best when freshly ground.

Sichuan peppercorns

Also called fargara, wild pepper, Chinese pepper and anise pepper, Sichuan peppercorns are an ancient spice known throughout China as 'flower peppers' because they resemble flower buds opening. Used extensively in Sichuan cooking, they are enjoyed in other parts of South-East Asia as well.

They are reddish-brown in colour with a strong, pungent odour that distinguishes them from the hotter black peppercorns with which they may be used interchangeably. Not related to peppers at all, they are the dried berries of a shrub that is a member of the prickly ash tree known as

fargara. Their smell reminds me of lavender, while their taste is sharp and slightly numbing to the tongue, with a clean lemon-wood spiciness and fragrance. It is not the peppercorns that make Sichuan cooking so hot, but the use of chilli pepper.

Sichuan peppercorns can be ground in a conventional peppermill but they should be roasted first in order to bring out their full flavour.

An inexpensive item, they are sold wrapped in cellophane or plastic bags by Chinese or Asian grocers. Avoid packets with dark seeds; the peppercorns should be a vibrant, rusty, reddish-brown colour. They are best when vacuum-packed, as they quickly lose their special aroma if left out too long. They will keep indefinitely if stored in a well-sealed container.

Combine them with other peppercorns for additional flavour. They can be used as part of a dry marinade with salt for grilled meat.

To roast Sichuan peppercorns

Heat a wok or heavy frying pan to a medium heat. Add the peppercorns (you can cook up to about 100g (4 oz) at a time) and stir-fry them for about 5 minutes or until they brown slightly and start to smoke. Remove the pan from the heat and allow to cool. Grind them in a peppermill or in a clean coffee grinder, or use a mortar and pestle. Sift the ground peppercorns through a fine mesh and discard any hard hulls. Seal tightly in a screw-top jar to store. Alternatively, keep the whole roasted peppercorns in a well-sealed container and grind them when required.

RICE

For the recipes in this book, the best rice to use is simple long-grain white rice, of which there are many varieties. I particularly like basmati or Thai rice (sometimes also known as Jasmine Fragrant rice). Both are superior varieties, which are drier and fluffier when cooked. They are now widely available. Avoid pre-cooked or 'easy-cook' rice as both these types have insufficient flavour and lack the necessary texture.

SAUCES AND PASTES

Asian cookery involves a number of tasty sauces and pastes, some light, some thick. They are essential to the authentic taste of dishes, and it is well worth making the effort to obtain them. Most are sold in bottles or tins by Asian or Chinese grocers and some supermarkets.

Tinned sauces, once opened, should be transferred to screw-top glass jars and kept in the refrigerator, where they will last indefinitely.

Chilli bean sauce

This thick dark sauce or paste, which is made from soyabeans, chillies and other seasonings, is very hot and spicy. It is usually available in the UK in jars from Chinese or Asian grocers. Be sure to seal the jar tightly after use and store in the larder or refrigerator. Do not confuse it with chilli sauce, which is a hotter, redder, thinner liquid made without beans and used mainly as a dipping sauce for cooked dishes.

Fish sauce

Fish sauce is also known as fish gravy or *nam pla*. This thin brown sauce, made from fermented salted fresh fish, usually anchovies, is sold bottled and has a noticeable fishy odour and salty taste. Fish sauce adds a special richness and quality to dishes, although cooking greatly diminishes its 'fishy' flavour. You may want to use it sparingly at first. Thai brands are especially good, with a less salty taste. It is an inexpensive ingredient, so get the best on offer.

Hoisin sauce

Hoisin sauce is part of the bean sauce family. It is a rich, thick, dark, brownish-red sauce, made from soya bean paste, garlic, vinegar, sugar, spices and other flavourings. It is at once sweet and spicy and its texture ranges from creamy thick to thin. In the West, it is often used mixed with some sesame oil and used as a sauce for Peking Duck.

Hoisin sauce is sold in tins and jars. It is sometimes also called barbecue sauce with hoisin sauce. However, check carefully, as there are barbecue sauces available that are quite different from hoisin sauce.

The best hoisin sauce comes from China under the brand name of Pearl River Bridge. Another good one from China is under the Ma Ling label. Other good brands come from Hong Kong, under the Amoy and Koon Chun Sauce Factory's label. If refrigerated, it should keep indefinitely.

Oyster sauce

This thick brown sauce is made from a concentrate of oysters cooked in soy sauce and brine. Despite its name, oyster sauce does not taste fishy. It has a rich flavour and is used not only in cooking but also as a condiment, diluted with a little oil, for vegetables, poultry and meat.

It is usually sold in bottles and can be obtained from Chinese or Asian grocers and supermarkets. I find it keeps best in the refrigerator. There is a version available for vegetarians, which is made with … just mushrooms.

Soy sauces

Soy sauce is an essential ingredient in Asian cooking. It is made from a mixture of soya beans, flour and water, which is fermented naturally and aged for some months. The liquid that is finally distilled is soy sauce.

There are two main types:

Light soy sauce – As the name implies, this is light in colour, but it is full of flavour and is the preferable choice for cooking. It is saltier than dark soy sauce. It is known by Chinese or Asian grocers as Superior Soy.

Dark soy sauce – This sauce is aged for much longer than light soy sauce, hence its darker, almost black colour. It is slightly thicker and stronger than light soy sauce and is more suitable for stews. I prefer it to light soy as a dipping sauce. It is known by Asian or Chinese grocers as Soy Superior Sauce. I like that: both versions are 'superior'.

Most soy sauces sold in supermarkets are dark soy. Chinese or Asian grocers sell both types and the quality is excellent. Check carefully, as the names are very similar.

Thai green curry paste

This is an intensely flavoured paste of herbs and spices used to flavour coconut curries, soups, and other dishes. Home-made curry paste is time-consuming to prepare. Fortunately, ready-made, high-quality Thai curry pastes are now available in most supermarkets. Thai green curry paste is made with fresh green chillies. Remember: green chillies are much stronger than red. If you prefer your dishes less 'hot', use Thai red curry paste, made with red dried chillies, which is less fiery.

SESAME SEEDS

These are dried seeds of the sesame herb. They have a pleasing nutty flavour and are rich in protein and minerals. Unhulled, the seeds range in colour from greyish-white to black, but once the hull is removed, the actual seeds are revealed to be tiny, somewhat flattened, cream-coloured and pointed at one end. Keep them in a glass jar in a cool dry place and they will last indefinitely.

Sesame paste is a rich, thick, creamy brown paste made from sesame seeds. It is used in both hot and cold dishes, and sold in jars, available from Asian grocers. If you cannot obtain sesame paste, use peanut butter which resembles it in texture. Don't confuse sesame paste, which is toasted, with puréed whole sesame seeds (tahini).

To make toasted sesame seeds

Heat a frying pan over high heat until it is hot. Add the sesame seeds and stir occasionally. Watch them closely, and when they begin to brown lightly, which will take about 3–5 minutes, give them a final stir before turning them onto a plate to cool. When they are completely cold, store them in an air-tight glass jar in a cool, dark place.

Alternatively, preheat the oven to 160°C, 325°F, gas mark 3. Spread the sesame seeds on a baking sheet, and roast them in the oven for about 10–15 minutes or until they are nicely toasted and lightly browned. Allow them to cool and then proceed as before.

SHAOXING RICE WINE

Rice wine has been an important component in Chinese cookery for centuries, and I believe the finest of its many varieties is produced in Shaoxing in Zhejiang Province in eastern China. It is made from glutinous rice, yeast and spring water. Chefs use it in marinades and sauces, as well as in cooking. Now readily available from Chinese or Asian grocers and some wine shops in the West, it should be kept tightly corked at room temperature.

Do not confuse this wine with *sake*, which is the Japanese version of rice wine and quite different. Western grape wines are not an adequate substitute for either. If not available, a good-quality, dry pale sherry can be substituted but cannot equal rice wine's rich, mellow taste.

SHALLOTS

Shallots are mild-flavoured members of the onion family and a very popular item in South-East Asia. They are small with copper-red skins and have a distinctive onion taste without being as overpowering as ordinary onions.

They are universally available, if a bit expensive, but a few go a long way. Keep them in a cool, dry place (not the refrigerator) and peel, slice or chop them as you would an onion. If all else fails you can use small, fresh yellow onions.

SHELLFISH

Four kinds of shellfish are used in these recipes: mussels, oysters, prawns and scallops.

Mussels

The season for mussels is usually between October to March. It is always a good idea to eat mussels the same day that you buy them, to make sure they are absolutely fresh. You can tell this by whether most of them are tightly closed or not; if a lot of them are open, don't buy them.

As soon as you get the mussels home, put them straight into a bowl of cold water. Throw away any that float to the top. Under a running cold tap, take a small knife and scrape off all the barnacles. Also cut or pull off the little hairy 'beards'. Discard any that are broken, and any that are open and don't close up again when you tap them sharply with a knife.

As you clean them, put them into another bowl of clean water and wash them in three or four changes of fresh water to get rid of any sand. Leave them in clean water until you are ready to cook. Always discard any mussel that hasn't opened after being cooked.

Oysters

Like mussels, oysters should only be bought if they are tightly closed. Using a stiff brush, scrub the shells to get rid of any sand. To open the oysters, hold the oyster in one hand, rounded shell upwards, and insert the tip of an oyster knife, or a knife with a short, strong blade, into the hinge. Twist the knife to prise it open and cut through the two hard muscles that lie on either side.

Prawns, raw

Most prawns previously available in Britain were sold cooked, either shelled or unshelled. However, it is increasingly possible to buy large uncooked prawns, known as Pacific or king prawns, usually in frozen form. These are most suitable for the recipes used in this book.

Most Asian or Chinese grocers, and many fishmongers and some supermarkets, stock them frozen and in the shell. Fresh prawns are occasionally available. In any case, frozen uncooked prawns are always preferable to cooked prawns, which in most cases are already overcooked and so will not absorb the virtues of any sauce you cook them in.

To peel prawns

First twist off the head and pull off the tail. It should then be quite easy to peel off the shell, and with it the tiny legs. If you are using large, uncooked king prawns, take a small sharp knife and make a shallow cut down the back of each prawn and remove the fine digestive cord that runs the length of the body. Wash the prawns well before you use them.

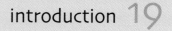

A trick for frozen raw prawns

After peeling and preparing the raw prawns as instructed above, rinse them three times in 1 tablespoon of salt to 1.2 litres (2 pints) cold water, changing the solution of salt and water each time. This process helps to firm the texture of the prawns and also gives them a crystalline clean taste.

Scallops

Always buy scallops live in the shell; if they are fresh, the shells will be closed. Some supermarkets sell scallops already prepared, so make sure they are plump and firm.

STAR ANISE

Star anise is a cluster of seed pods that together form the shape of an eight-pointed star. It is similar in flavour and fragrance to common aniseed, but it is more robust and liquorice-like. Indeed, the essential oil of star anise is used in the West for the making of liqueurs and other aniseed-flavoured food products.

Star anise is an essential ingredient of five-spice powder and is widely used in braised dishes, to which it imparts a rich taste and fragrance. It is sold in plastic packs by Chinese or Asian grocers, and should be stored in a tightly covered jar in a cool, dry place.

SUGAR

Sugar has been used – sparingly – in savoury dishes in South-East Asia for centuries. Properly employed, it helps balance the various flavours of sauces and other dishes.

Chinese rock sugar

Chinese rock sugar has a rich and more subtle flavour than refined granulated sugar. It also gives a good lustre or glaze to braised dishes and sauces.

You can buy it in Chinese or Asian groceries, where it is usually sold in packets. You may need to break the slabs or lumps into smaller pieces with a wooden mallet or rolling pin. If you cannot obtain it, you can substitute white sugar or coffee sugar crystals (the amber, chunky kind). Alternatively, mix light brown sugar with an equal part of molasses.

VINEGARS

Vinegars are widely used in Asian cooking. Unlike Western kinds, they are usually made from rice. There are many varieties, ranging in flavour from the spicy and slightly tart to the sweet and pungent.

Two kinds of rice vinegar are used in these recipes: white and black. Both can be found in Asian grocers and supermarkets. They are sold in bottles and will keep indefinitely.

If you cannot get them, you can substitute cider vinegar. Malt vinegar can be used, but it is stronger and more acidic. Never simply substitute Western white vinegar for rice vinegar: the contrast is too great.

TECHNIQUES

CUTTING TECHNIQUES

Slicing

This is the conventional method of slicing food. Hold the food firmly on the chopping board with one hand and slice the food straight down into very thin slices. Meat is always sliced across the grain to break up the fibres and to make it more tender when it is cooked. If you use a cleaver rather than a knife for this, hold the cleaver with your index finger over the far side of the top of the cleaver and your thumb on the side nearest you to guide the cutting edge firmly. Hold the food with your other hand, turning your fingers under for safety. Your knuckles should act as a guide for the blade.

Diagonal slicing

This technique is used for cutting vegetables such as asparagus, carrots or spring onions. The purpose is to expose more of the surface of the vegetable for quicker cooking. Angle the knife or cleaver at a slant and cut.

Roll-cutting

This is rather like diagonal slicing, but is used for larger vegetables such as courgettes, large carrots, aubergines and Chinese white radish (mooli). As with diagonal slicing, this technique allows more of the surface of the vegetable to be exposed to the heat, thereby speeding up the cooking time.

Begin by making one diagonal cut at one end of the vegetable. Then turn it 180 degrees and make the next diagonal cut. Continue in this way until you have sliced the entire vegetable into evenly sized, diamond-shaped chunks.

Shredding

This is the process by which food is cut into thin, fine, matchstick-like shreds. First cut the food into slices and then pile several slices on top of each other and cut them lengthways into fine strips. Some foods, particularly meat and chicken breasts, are easier to shred if they are first stiffened slightly in the freezer for about 20 minutes.

Dicing

This is a simple technique of cutting food into small cubes or dice. The food should first be cut into slices. Stack the slices and cut them again *lengthways* into sticks, just as you would for shredding (above). Stack the strips or sticks and cut *crossways* into evenly sized cubes or dice.

Mincing

This is a fine-chopping technique. Chefs use two cleavers to mince, rapidly chopping with them in unison for fast results. One cleaver or knife is easier for the less expert, although the process will of course take a little longer!

First slice the food and then, using a sharp knife or cleaver, rapidly chop it until it is rather spread out over the chopping board. Scrape it into a pile and chop again, and continue chopping until the food reaches the desired state. You may find it easier to hold the knife or cleaver by the top of the blade (rather than by the handle) with two hands, as though you were chopping parsley. A food processor may also be used

for this but be careful not to over-mince the food or you will lose out on texture and taste.

COOKING TECHNIQUES

Blanching

This involves putting food into boiling water or into moderately hot oil for a few minutes to cook it briefly but not entirely. It is a sort of softening-up process to prepare food for final cooking. Harder vegetables, such as broccoli or carrots, are sometimes blanched in boiling water for several minutes, then plunged into cold water to arrest the cooking process. In such cases, blanching usually precedes stir-frying to finish the cooking.

Deep-frying

This is one of the most important techniques in Chinese cooking. The trick is to regulate the heat so that the surface of the food is sealed but does not brown so fast that the food is uncooked inside. Although deep-fried food must not be greasy, the process does require a lot of oil.

The Chinese use a wok for deep-frying, which requires rather less oil than a deep-fat fryer, but it may be best to avoid using a wok to deep-fry unless you are very sure of it. If you do choose to use your wok, make certain that it is fully secure on its stand before adding the oil and on no account leave the wok unsupervised.

Some points to bear in mind when deep-frying:
- Wait for the oil to get hot enough before adding the food. The oil should give off a haze and almost produce little wisps of smoke when it is the right temperature, but you can test it by dropping in a small piece of food. If the oil bubbles all over, then it is sufficiently hot. Adjust the heat to prevent the oil from actually smoking or overheating.
- Food that is to be deep-fried should first be dried thoroughly with kitchen paper. This will prevent splattering. If the food is in a marinade, remove it with a slotted spoon and let it drain before putting it into the oil. If you are using batter, make sure all the excess batter drips off before adding the food to the hot oil.

- Oil used for deep-frying can be reused (see page 15). Label it according to what food you have cooked in the oil and only reuse it for the same thing.
- When food is deep-fried, this often has to be done in several batches, because if you deep-fry too much food at once, it will cool the oil, preventing it from cooking the food properly and crisply. You don't need to worry about keeping one batch hot while you cook another because one benefit of wok cookery is that most food cooked in it will remain quite hot for at least 20 minutes or so.

Steaming

Steaming has been used by the Chinese for thousands of years. Steamed foods are cooked by a gentle moist heat which must circulate freely in order to cook the food. It is an excellent method for bringing out subtle flavours and so is particularly wonderful for fish. It is also one of the best methods for reheating food since it warms it without cooking it further and without drying it out.

- You can use the wok as a steamer. Put about 5cm (2 in) water in a wok. Then put a metal or wooden rack into the wok. Bring the water to simmering point and put the food to be steamed onto a heatproof plate. Lower the plate onto the rack and cover the wok tightly with a wok lid. Check the water level from time to time and replenish it with hot water when necessary. If you do not have a metal or wooden rack, you could use a small empty tin to support the plate of food. Remember that the food needs to remain above the water level and must not get wet. The water level should always be at least 2.5cm (1 in) below the edge of the food plate.
- You can use a bamboo steamer inside a wok. For this you need a large bamboo steamer about 25.5cm (10 in) wide. Put about 5cm (2 in) water in a wok. Bring it to simmering point. Put the bamboo steamer containing the food into the wok where it should rest safely, perched on the sloping sides. Cover the steamer with its lid and steam the food until cooked. Replenish the water as required.

Stir-frying

This is the most famous of all Chinese cooking techniques and it is possibly the most tricky, since success with it depends upon having all the required ingredients prepared, measured out and immediately on hand, and on having a good source of fierce heat. Its advantage is that, properly executed, stir-fried foods can be cooked in minutes in very little oil so they retain their natural flavours and textures. It is important that stir-fried foods are not overcooked or greasy.

Once you have mastered this technique, you will find that it becomes almost second nature. Using a wok is definitely an advantage when stir-frying, as its shape not only conducts the heat well but its high sides enable you to toss and stir ingredients rapidly, keeping them moving while cooking.

Having prepared all the ingredients, the steps are:
- Heat the wok until it is very hot *before* adding the oil. This prevents food sticking and will ensure an even heat. Add the oil and, using a metal spatula or long-handled spoon, distribute it evenly over the surface. It should be very hot indeed – almost smoking – before you add the next ingredient unless you are going on to flavour the oil.
- If you are flavouring the oil with garlic, spring onions, ginger, dried red chillies or salt, do not wait for the oil to get so hot that it is almost smoking. If you do, these ingredients will burn and become bitter. Toss them quickly in the oil for a few seconds. In some recipes these flavourings may be removed and discarded before cooking proceeds.
- Now add the ingredients as described in the recipe and proceed to stir-fry by tossing them over the surface of the wok with the metal spatula or long-handled spoon. If you are stir-frying meat, let each side rest for just a few seconds before continuing to stir. Keep moving the food from the centre of the wok to the sides. Stir-frying is usually accompanied by quite a lot of splattering because of the high temperature at which the food must be cooked.
- Some stir-fried dishes are thickened with a mixture of cornflour and cold water. To avoid getting a lumpy sauce,

be sure to remove the wok from the heat before you add the cornflour mixture, which must be thoroughly blended before it is added. The sauce can then be returned to the heat and thickened.

Marinating

Marinating is a process in which raw meat or poultry is steeped for a time in a liquid such as soy sauce, rice wine or sherry and cornflour to improve its flavour and to tenderise it. Once marination is complete, the food is usually lifted out of the marinade with a slotted spoon before it is cooked.

In Chinese cooking, marinades vary: some foods are meant to be left in the marinade for a period (usually a minimum of 20 minutes); some are used immediately. Some need to be refrigerated; others can remain at room temperature. Marinades that require refrigeration do not need to be brought back to room temperature before cooking.

Zesting

The best and quickest way to obtain zest from citrus fruit such as lemons or limes is to use a zester: about the size of a vegetable knife, it has a broad head with a row of small sharp-edged holes. You simply pull this across the skin of the fruit and the zest is sliced off in long thin strips, minus the bitter pith. An alternative method is to carefully peel the skin off the fruit with a sharp knife, leaving behind the white pith. Then chop the peel finely.

BASIC RECIPES

BASIC HOME-MADE CHICKEN STOCK

Chicken stock is the all-purpose base for soups and sauces. Its chief ingredient is inexpensive; it is light and delicious; and it marries well with other foods, enhancing and sustaining them. I find that the richer stocks made with ham or pork bones are heavier and not quite to my taste. This simple recipe for chicken stock reflects what I believe works best for any dish.

Remember that stock prepared in this way can also be served just as it is, as a clear soup.

Many of the commercially prepared canned or cubed (dried) stocks are of inferior quality, being either too salty or containing additives and colourings that adversely affect your health as well as the natural taste of good food. However, many supermarkets now carry fresh stock that is quite acceptable, usually without the additives.

Stock does take time to prepare but it is easy to make your own – and when home-made, it is the best.

Your first step on the path to success with wok cooking must be to prepare and maintain an ample supply of good chicken stock, as many recipes in this book rely on it for just the right finish. I prefer to make it in large quantities at a time

and freeze it. However, you may find it useful to freeze it in 600ml (1 pint) containers or even smaller, if you are likely to need small quantities at a time. Here are several important points to keep in mind when making stock:

- Good stock requires meat to give it richness and flavour. It is therefore necessary to use at least some chicken meat, if not a whole bird.
- The stock should never boil. If it does, it will become cloudy and the fat will be incorporated into the liquid. Flavour and digestibility come with a clear stock.
- Use a deep heavy saucepan so the liquid covers all the solids and evaporation is slow.
- Simmer slowly and skim the stock regularly. Be patient; you will reap rewards each time you prepare meals on the basis of this delicate stock.
- Strain the finished stock well through several layers of cheesecloth or a fine-mesh strainer.
- Let the stock cool thoroughly, then refrigerate. Remove any solidified fat before freezing it.

MAKES ABOUT 3.4 LITRES (6 PINTS)
PREPARATION TIME: 15 MINUTES
COOKING TIME: 3–4 HOURS
My method of careful skimming ensures a clear stock, essential for good soups and sauces. Remember to save all your uncooked chicken bones and carcasses for stock. They can be frozen until you are ready to use them. If you find the amount in this recipe too large for your needs, make half.

2kg (4½ lb) raw chicken bones, such as backs, feet, wings
750g (1½ lb) chicken pieces, such as wings, thighs,
    drumsticks
3.4 litres (6 pints) cold water
small piece fresh ginger, 5 x 6cm (2 x 3 in)
9 whole spring onions
1 head whole garlic, unpeeled
2 teaspoons salt
1 teaspoon whole black peppercorns

1 Put the chicken bones and chicken pieces into a very large pot. (The bones can be put in either frozen or defrosted.) Cover them with the water and bring to simmering point.

2 Meanwhile peel the ginger and cut into diagonal slices, 5 x 1cm (2 x ½ in). Remove the green tops of the spring onions. Separate the head of garlic into cloves, without peeling them.

3 Using a large, flat spoon, skim off the foam as it rises from the bones. Watch the heat as the stock should never boil. Keep skimming until the stock looks clear. This can take between 20 to 40 minutes. Do not stir or disturb the stock.

4 Now turn the heat down to a low simmer. Add the ginger, spring onions, garlic, salt and peppercorns. Simmer the stock on a very low heat for between 2 and 4 hours, skimming any fat off the top at least twice during this time.

5 Strain the stock through several layers of dampened cheesecloth or through a very fine-mesh strainer, then let it cool thoroughly. When it is cold, remove any fat that has risen to the top. It is now ready to be used at once or transferred to containers and frozen.

BASIC HOME-MADE VEGETARIAN STOCK

Vegetarian cooking presents a problem when it comes to stock. In the absence of poultry, fish or meat, it is difficult to prepare a truly rich stock, the foundation of any cuisine. But, of course, it is the animal fat that makes it 'rich', and for many people that is too high a price to pay.

Although vegetable stocks tend to lack robustness they can still serve our purpose. One of the best vegetarian stocks I have ever sampled was that of Chef Norbert Kostner, the Executive Chef of the famed Oriental Hotel in Bangkok. Although Norbert is from Switzerland, he has lived for several decades in Bangkok. He has adopted and adapted the fine nuances of Asian tastes and flavours. He kindly shared with me some of his ideas for his superb vegetable stock and I have made a version suitable for home kitchens. To get assertive flavours, he suggested a ratio of 3 litres (5 pints) of water to at least 5kg (11¼ lb) of vegetables.

Although the use of such a quantity of vegetables may sound extravagant, we must remember that we are distilling essences here and, moreover, it is a fraction of what it would cost to make a meat stock.

I have found that browning the vegetables in the oven *before* simmering helps to impart flavours to the stock.

Since this vegetable stock recipe is easy to make, I suggest that you prepare a fairly large quantity, as it freezes quite well and is essential to have on hand. Again, if you don't have the time to make stock from scratch, there are some acceptable commercial vegetarian stocks available now.

If you find the amount in this recipe too large for your needs, make half.

MAKES ABOUT 2.75 LITRES (5 PINTS)
PREPARATION TIME: 35 MINUTES
COOKING TIME: 3 HOURS

50g (2 oz) Chinese dried mushrooms
1kg (2¼ lb) carrots, peeled
4 celery stalks, trimmed
1kg (2 lb) onions, peeled
1kg (2 lb) mooli (Chinese white radish), peeled
225g (8 oz) cucumber, peeled, halved lengthways and seeded
1kg (2 lb) tomatoes
4 leeks
225g (8 oz) shallots
small piece fresh ginger, 5 x 6cm (2 x 3 in)
6 whole spring onions, trimmed
10 unpeeled and crushed garlic cloves
2 tablespoons black peppercorns
1 tablespoon Sichuan peppercorns (optional)
2 tablespoons salt
2.75 litres (5 pints) water
3 tablespoons light soy sauce

1 Soak the mushrooms in warm water for 20 minutes, then drain them, reserving the liquid. Squeeze out and reserve any excess liquid from the mushrooms and strain. Set aside. Coarsely chop them, using both caps and stems.

2 Coarsely chop the carrots, celery, onions, mooli, cucumber and tomatoes. Wash the leeks, discard the green part and coarsely chop the white portion. Wash again to get rid of any remaining grit. Peel the shallots but leave them whole. Peel the ginger and cut into slices 5 x 1cm (2 x ½ in).

3 Preheat the oven to 220°C, 450°F, gas mark 8. Place on a baking tray the spring onions, ginger, garlic, shallots, mushrooms, carrots, celery, onions, mooli and leeks, and brown in the oven for 20 minutes.

4 Add the cucumbers and tomatoes and brown for another 8 minutes. Turn the vegetables into a very large saucepan and add the peppercorns, salt, water and soy sauce. Cover and bring to simmering point.

5 Using a large, flat spoon, skim off any foam as it rises to the top. It will take about 10–20 minutes for all the foam to rise.

6 Bring the stock to the boil, then turn the heat down to a moderate simmer and cook for about 2 hours. Skim off the foam from time to time.

7 Strain the stock through a large colander and then through a very fine-mesh strainer. Allow it to cool thoroughly. It is now ready to be used or transferred to containers and frozen.

STEAMED RICE

Steaming rice is a simple, straightforward and efficient technique. The secret of preparing rice without it being sticky is to cook it first in an uncovered pan at a high heat until most of the water has evaporated. Then the heat should be turned very low, the pot covered, and the rice cooked slowly in the remaining steam.

A couple of important rules to remember:

- The water should be at a level 2.5cm (1 in) above the surface of the rice; too much water means gummy rice. Recipes on commercial packets generally recommend too much water.
- Never uncover the pot once the simmering process has begun; time the process and wait.

SERVES 4
PREPARATION TIME: 5 MINUTES
COOKING TIME: 35 MINUTES

Enough long-grain white rice to fill a glass measuring jug
   to the 400ml (14 fl oz) level
600ml (1 pint) water

1 Put the rice into a large bowl and wash it in several changes of water until the water becomes clear. Drain and transfer to a heavy saucepan with the water. Make sure the water comes to 2.5cm (1 in) above the surface of the rice. If necessary, adjust the amount of water.

2 Bring the water to the boil and continue boiling until most of the surface liquid has evaporated. This should take about 15 minutes. The surface of the rice should be pitted with small indentations.

3 At this point, cover the saucepan with a very tight-fitting lid, turn the heat down as low as possible and let the rice cook undisturbed for 15 minutes. Remove from the heat.

4 There is no need to 'fluff' the rice. Just let it rest, covered, for 5 minutes before serving it.

starters and appetisers

This popular starter from Hong Kong uses raw green prawns. You can find frozen raw prawns that are shelled and ready-peeled in the supermarkets these days. In this recipe, the prawns are not peeled before being cooked, because this keeps them moist and succulent.

salt and pepper prawns

450g (1 lb) small raw unpeeled prawns, fresh or frozen
2 tablespoons salt
450ml (14 fl oz) groundnut (peanut) oil

SEASONING
2 fresh chillies, seeded and coarsely chopped
Maldon sea salt, to taste
1 teaspoon roasted and ground Sichuan peppercorns or freshly ground black pepper
1 teaspoon sugar
2 tablespoons coarsely chopped garlic
2 tablespoons finely chopped spring onions

GARNISH
handful fresh coriander sprigs (optional)

1 If using frozen prawns, defrost fully. Fill a large bowl with cold water, add 1 tablespoon of salt and gently wash the prawns in the salted water. Drain, and repeat the process, using a fresh bowl of water and the remaining salt. Drain again. Remove the feathery legs from the prawns and discard. Blot dry with kitchen paper.

2 In a small bowl, combine the ingredients for the seasoning and set aside.

3 Heat a wok over high heat until it is hot. Add the oil, and when it is very hot and slightly smoking, add the prawns and deep-fry for about 1 minute or until they are slightly pink. Remove them immediately with a slotted spoon and set aside to drain well on kitchen paper.

4 Pour off all the oil and reheat the wok. When it is hot and slightly smoking, add the seasoning mixture and stir-fry for 30 seconds.

5 Return the prawns to the wok and stir-fry over high heat for about 2 minutes or until the spices have thoroughly coated their outer shells.

6 Turn onto a warm serving platter, garnish with the coriander if using and serve at once. This quick starter can be also be served as a main course in itself.

I love these more-ish, delectable starters. They are very easy to make and quick to cook. Ideal for a party, especially when you are in a hurry.

crispy curried chicken

450g (1 lb) boneless, skinless chicken thighs

cornflour, for dusting

450ml (15 fl oz) groundnut (peanut) oil

MARINADE

salt and freshly ground black pepper, to taste

1½ tablespoons Madras curry powder

P Can be prepared ahead: cover and refrigerate for up to 1 hour.

1 Cut the chicken thighs into 7.5cm (3 in) pieces. In a large bowl, combine the ingredients for the marinade. Add the chicken, mix well and marinate for at least 10 minutes at room temperature. Drain, discarding the marinade. **P**

2 Dust the chicken with the cornflour, shaking off any excess.

3 Heat a wok over high heat until it is hot, then add the oil. Turn the heat down to moderate and deep-fry the chicken for 5 minutes or until golden brown. Remove with a slotted spoon and drain on kitchen paper.

4 Turn onto a warm platter and serve at once.

One of my secret weapons for fast cooking is soy sauce. When used as a marinade, it seeps quickly into the food, flavouring it in a very special way. In just 20 minutes, it transforms ordinary chicken into something special.

soy sauce chicken

450g (1 lb) boneless, skinless chicken
thighs
cornflour, for dusting
450ml (15 fl oz) groundnut (peanut) oil

MARINADE
3 tablespoons light soy sauce
1 tablespoon Shaoxing rice wine or dry
sherry
2 teaspoons ginger juice (see page 13)
salt and freshly ground black pepper, to taste

P Can be prepared ahead: cover and
refrigerate for up to 1 hour.

1 Cut the chicken thighs into 7.5cm (3 in) pieces. In a large bowl, combine the ingredients for the marinade. Add the chicken, mix well and marinate for 20 minutes at room temperature. Drain, discarding the marinade. P

2 Dust the chicken with the cornflour, shaking off any excess.

3 Heat a wok over high heat until it is hot, then add the oil. Turn down the heat to moderate and deep-fry the chicken for 5 minutes or until golden brown. Remove with a slotted spoon and drain on kitchen paper.

4 Turn onto a warm platter and serve at once.

Cooked in large quantities, this makes an unusual party dish. The first part of the recipe (up to the end of stage 2) can be prepared a day ahead. Served at room temperature without the last-minute frying, the chicken wings make wonderful picnic fare.

five-spice chicken wings

675g (1 lb) chicken wings

3 garlic cloves, peeled and crushed

1 piece fresh ginger 2.5cm (1 in) thick, unpeeled and crushed

4 whole spring onions

50ml (2 fl oz) dark soy sauce

2 tablespoons light soy sauce

2 tablespoons Shaoxing rice wine or dry sherry

salt and freshly ground black pepper, to taste

2 tablespoons sugar

50ml (2 fl oz) water

2 teaspoons five-spice powder

cornflour, for dusting

450ml (15 fl oz) groundnut (peanut) oil

P Can be prepared ahead: cover and refrigerate for up to 24 hours.

1 Put the chicken wings into a wok, together with the garlic, ginger, spring onions, soy sauces, rice wine or sherry, salt, pepper, sugar and water. Bring to simmering point. Then reduce the heat to very low, cover and simmer for 10 minutes.

2 Turn the wings over and simmer for another 10 minutes. Remove with a slotted spoon, drain on kitchen paper and allow to cool thoroughly. This will keep in the fridge for up to 24 hours. P

3 Mix the five-spice powder with a little salt and set aside.

4 Dust the chicken with cornflour, shaking off any excess. Divide into two batches. The wings need to be cooked in batches because if you deep-fry too much food at once, it will cool the oil, preventing it from cooking the food properly and crisply.

5 Heat a wok over high heat until it is hot, then add the oil. Turn the heat down to moderate and deep-fry the first batch for 5 minutes or until golden brown. Remove with a slotted spoon and drain on kitchen paper. Repeat for the second batch.

6 Turn the chicken wings onto a warm platter, sprinkle with the five-spice powder mix and serve at once.

SERVES 4

PREPARATION TIME: 10 MINUTES

COOKING TIME: 10 MINUTES

The versatility of chicken is one reason why it is so popular with cooks looking for tasty but quick starters. Here the chicken is marinated, then covered with sesame seeds and deep-fried. A savoury way to begin any meal. As before, the chicken needs to be deep-fried in batches, to ensure that it cooks properly and crisply.

sesame seed chicken

225g (8 oz) boneless, skinless chicken breasts
cornflour, for dusting
2 egg whites, lightly beaten
6 tablespoons raw white sesame seeds
450ml (15 fl oz) groundnut (peanut) oil

MARINADE
1 tablespoon light soy sauce
1½ tablespoons Shaoxing rice wine or dry sherry
salt, to taste
1 teaspoon sugar
1 teaspoon sesame oil
2 teaspoons lemon juice

1 Cut the chicken on the diagonal into thin strips about 7.5cm (3 in) long. In a medium-sized bowl, combine the marinade ingredients. Add the chicken and mix well to coat. Drain, discarding the marinade.

2 Dust the chicken with cornflour, shaking off any excess. Then dip in the egg whites and finally in the sesame seeds. Divide into two or three batches.

3 Heat a wok over high heat until it is hot, then add the oil. Turn the heat down to moderate and deep-fry the chicken, one batch at a time, for 5 minutes or until golden brown. Remove when cooked and drain on kitchen paper. Repeat for the remaining batches.

4 Arrange on a warm platter and serve at once.

SERVES 4

PREPARATION TIME: 35 MINUTES

COOKING TIME: 3 MINUTES

I love these tasty, quick and easy starters. They are a delicious way to start any meal. Make sure that you use raw prawns for this recipe.

Burmese prawns

450g (1 lb) raw unpeeled prawns, fresh or frozen

1 tablespoon salt

2 tablespoons groundnut (peanut) oil

MARINADE

2 tablespoons finely chopped garlic

½ teaspoon chilli powder (optional)

2 tablespoons lime juice

salt and freshly ground black pepper, to taste

2 teaspoons turmeric

2 eggs, beaten

2 teaspoons sesame oil

P Can be prepared ahead: cover the prawns and refrigerate for up to 2 hours.

1 If using frozen prawns, defrost thoroughly. Peel the prawns and discard the shells. Using a small sharp knife, remove the fine digestive cord. Wash the prawns in a bowl of cold water to which you have added 1 tablespoon salt. Drain and pat dry with kitchen paper.

2 In a large bowl, combine the marinade ingredients and mix well. Add the prawns and marinate for 30 minutes at room temperature. Drain, discarding the marinade. P

3 Heat a wok over high heat until it is hot. Add the oil, and when it is very hot and slightly smoking, add the prawns. Stir-fry for about 3 minutes or until pink.

4 Turn onto a warm platter and serve at once.

These are the perfect starters – tasty, light and easy to make. The best part is that you don't even have to be a vegetarian to enjoy them.

savoury mushrooms

225g (8 oz) fresh shiitake or large button
   mushrooms
salt, to taste
3 tablespoons plain flour
1 tablespoon Madras curry powder
3 tablespoons groundnut (peanut) oil

1 Pick over the mushrooms, choosing the largest and best-looking ones. If you are using fresh shiitake mushrooms, trim off the stems and discard. Rinse in cold water and pat dry with kitchen paper. If you are using large button mushrooms, trim off the stems and discard. Rinse well in cold water and pat dry with kitchen paper.

2 Sprinkle salt lightly on both sides of each mushroom.

3 In a small bowl, mix together the flour and curry powder. Dust the mixture over each mushroom cap, shaking off any excess.

4 Heat a wok over high heat until it is hot. Add the oil, and when it is hot and slightly smoking, turn the heat to low. Add the mushrooms and gently pan-fry them, undisturbed, for about 2 minutes on each side.

5 Turn onto a warm platter, sprinkle with a little more salt and serve at once.

SERVES 4–6

PREPARATION TIME: 25 MINUTES

COOKING TIME: 5 MINUTES

I often think that chicken livers are a neglected but delicious food. They cook quickly and are quite economical. Here they are simply marinated and rapidly seared in the wok. The secret is not to overcook them but to leave them slightly pink and moist.

delectable chicken livers

450g (1 lb) fresh chicken livers
1 tablespoon salt
3 spring onions
3 tablespoons groundnut (peanut) oil

MARINADE
3 tablespoons light soy sauce
2 tablespoons ginger juice (see page 13)
1 tablespoon Mirin (Japanese sweet rice wine) or Shaoxing rice wine or dry sherry
2 teaspoons sesame oil
1½ tablespoons sugar

P Can be prepared ahead: cover the livers and spring onions and refrigerate separately for up to 6 hours.

1 Cut the chicken livers in half. Put in a large bowl and add the salt. Mix together well. Add enough water to cover the livers and leave to soak for 10 minutes. Then rinse, drain well and pat dry with kitchen paper. Discard the water.

2 In a medium-sized bowl, combine all the marinade ingredients. Add the chicken livers and mix well. Marinate for 15 minutes at room temperature. Drain, reserving the marinade.

3 Cut the spring onions into 5cm (2 in) pieces. P

4 Heat a wok until it is hot and add the oil. When the oil is very hot and slightly smoking, add the livers and stir-fry for 3 minutes.

5 Then add the reserved marinade and the spring onions. Continue to stir-fry for 2 minutes. Remove from the heat and allow to cool.

6 When the livers are cool enough to handle, thread them on bamboo skewers alternately with the spring onion pieces, taking care to put no more than 3 or 4 livers on each skewer.

7 Arrange on a warm platter and serve at once.

SERVES 4

PREPARATION TIME: 3 MINUTES

COOKING TIME: 25 MINUTES

These subtly flavoured nuts are easy to make and are finished off in the oven. The exotic taste of curry adds a new twist, which makes them quite irresistible.

curried cashew nuts

2 tablespoons groundnut (peanut) oil
2 tablespoons coarsely chopped garlic
225g (8 oz) raw cashew nuts
1 tablespoon light soy sauce
1 tablespoon Madras curry powder
salt and freshly ground black pepper, to taste
½ teaspoon five-spice powder

1 Preheat the oven to 140°C, 275°F, gas mark 1.

2 Heat a wok until it is hot, then add the oil. When the oil is moderately hot, add the garlic and cashew nuts, and stir-fry for 30 seconds or until lightly brown. Now add the soy sauce and stir-fry over moderate heat for about 2 minutes or the liquid has evaporated.

3 Then add the curry powder, salt, pepper and five-spice powder and mix well so that the nuts are thoroughly coated with the spices. Remove the nuts with a slotted spoon and spread on a baking tray.

4 Cook in the oven for about 15–20 minutes or until lightly brown. The nuts will be crisp once they begin to cool.

5 Turn onto a platter and serve immediately.

soups

SERVES 4
PREPARATION TIME: 10 MINUTES
COOKING TIME: 15 MINUTES

Lemongrass is perfect for quick cooking as it can easily transform ordinary soup into something special without any extra effort. Its uplifting, refreshing flavour enhances any dish.

lemongrass chicken soup

100g (4 oz) boneless, skinless chicken breasts
2 stalks fresh lemongrass
1.2 litres (2 pints) home-made chicken stock (see page 23) or quality store-bought fresh stock
1 tablespoon finely chopped ginger
salt and freshly ground black pepper, to taste
2 tablespoons light soy sauce
2 spring onions, finely shredded
handful fresh coriander sprigs

1 Cut the chicken into thin slices about 7.5cm (3 in).

2 Peel the lemongrass stalk to the tender whitish centre and crush it with the flat of a knife. Then cut it into 7.5cm (3 in) pieces.

3 In a wok, bring the stock to simmering point and add the lemongrass. Turn the heat to low, cover and simmer for 10 minutes. Remove the lemongrass with a slotted spoon and discard.

4 Then add the chicken slices, ginger, salt, pepper and soy sauce. Cook gently for another 3 minutes.

5 Finally, stir in the spring onions and coriander.

6 Ladle into a large soup tureen or individual bowls and serve immediately.

SERVES 4

PREPARATION TIME: 15 MINUTES

COOKING TIME: 10 MINUTES

This is a fast and satisfying soup. If you are new to them, see the Ingredients section for instructions about using beanthread noodles.

beanthread noodle beef soup

50g (2 oz) beanthread (transparent) noodles

1.2 litres (2 pints) home-made chicken stock (see page 23) or quality store-bought fresh stock

175g (6 oz) minced beef

1 tablespoon light soy sauce

2 teaspoons dark soy sauce

1 tablespoon Shaoxing rice wine or dry sherry

2 teaspoons sugar

salt and freshly ground black pepper, to taste

2 teaspoons cornflour, mixed with 1 tablespoon cold water

2 teaspoons sesame oil

1 Soak the noodles in hot water for 15 minutes. When soft, drain well and discard the water. Cut into 7.5cm (3 in) lengths, using scissors or a knife. Set aside.

2 Pour the stock into a wok and bring to the boil. Add the beef, beanthread noodles, soy sauces, rice wine or sherry, sugar, salt and pepper and turn the heat down to moderate. Gently simmer for about 4 minutes.

3 Add the cornflour mixture and continue to cook, stirring constantly, for another 3 minutes or until the soup has slightly thickened.

4 Finally, add the sesame oil and give the soup several good stirs.

5 Turn into a soup tureen or individual bowls and serve at once.

SERVES 4

PREPARATION TIME: 10 MINUTES

COOKING TIME: 15 MINUTES

This is a fast version of a Thai-style soup that is easy to make and extremely tasty. Perfect for a dinner party too. If you like your food really spicy, include a teaspoon or two of chilli powder.

spicy prawn soup

225g (8 oz) raw unpeeled prawns, fresh or frozen

1.2 litres (2 pints) home-made chicken stock (see page 23) or quality store-bought fresh stock

1 or 2 fresh red chillies, seeded and finely shredded

salt and freshly ground black pepper, to taste

2 tablespoons fish sauce or light soy sauce

1 tablespoon lime zest

2 tablespoons lime juice

1–2 teaspoons chilli powder (optional)

handful fresh coriander sprigs

1 If using frozen prawns, defrost thoroughly. Peel the prawns and discard the shells. Using a small sharp knife, remove the fine digestive cord. Wash the prawns in cold water, rinse well and pat dry with kitchen paper.

2 In a wok, bring the stock to simmering point. Add the chillies, salt, pepper, fish sauce or soy sauce, lime zest and lime juice. If you like it spicy, add the chilli powder. Simmer for another 3 minutes.

3 Add the prawns, cover the wok and remove from the heat. Allow to stand, covered, for 10 minutes.

4 Finally, stir in the coriander.

5 Ladle into a large soup tureen or individual bowls and serve immediately.

SERVES 2–4

PREPARATION TIME: 25 MINUTES

COOKING TIME: 15 MINUTES

This mouth-watering, satisfying Thai-inspired soup is not only healthy but a meal in itself. Its distinctive, delicious taste will appeal even to inveterate meat eaters. Use vegetarian stock if you want to make this dish completely vegetarian.

Thai-style rice noodles in soup

175g (6 oz) flat dried rice noodles,
  rice vermicelli or rice sticks
1.2 litres (2 pints) home-made chicken or
  vegetarian stock (see pages 23–6)
  or quality store-bought fresh stock
salt, to taste
1 tablespoon light soy sauce
1 tablespoon lime juice
2 fresh red chillies, seeded and shredded
2 teaspoons sugar
1 tablespoon groundnut (peanut) oil
3 tablespoons coarsely chopped garlic

GARNISH
175g (6 oz) fresh beansprouts
3 tablespoons finely chopped spring
  onions
handful fresh coriander sprigs

1 Soak the rice noodles in a bowl of hot water for 25 minutes. When soft, drain well in a colander or sieve and set aside. Discard the water.

2 Bring the stock to simmering point in a large saucepan. Add the salt, soy sauce, lime juice, chillies and sugar. Continue to simmer for 10 minutes. Then add the rice noodles and simmer for another 2 minutes.

3 Heat a wok over high heat until it is hot. Add the oil, and when it is moderately hot, add the garlic and stir-fry rapidly until light brown. Remove immediately and drain on kitchen paper.

4 Turn the soup into a tureen or individual bowls. Sprinkle with the fried garlic, garnish with the beansprouts, spring onions and coriander, and serve at once.

Whenever I am in a hurry, this is my vegetarian standby. The 'eggflower' motif – lovely strands of lace-like white of egg – is a common one in South-East Asia. Vegetables are rarely assertive in flavour, but here, the crushed lemongrass stalks and ginger give the soup a tangy and refreshing taste.

vegetarian eggflower soup

2 stalks fresh lemongrass

1.2 litres (2 pints) home-made vegetarian stock (see page 24) or quality store-bought fresh stock

salt and freshly ground black pepper, to taste

2 teaspoons sugar

1 tablespoon fresh lemon juice

1 egg white

2 teaspoons sesame oil

GARNISH

handful fresh coriander sprigs

3 tablespoons finely chopped spring onions

1 With the flat of a cleaver or a heavy knife, crush the lemongrass stalks.

2 Put the stock in a wok and bring to simmering point. Add the lemongrass, salt, pepper, sugar and lemon juice and stir to mix well. Simmer gently for 10 minutes. Remove the lemongrass stalks and discard.

3 In a small bowl, beat the egg white lightly and combine with the sesame oil. Pour into the stock in a very slow, thin stream. Using a chopstick or fork, pull the egg gently into strands. (I find that stirring the egg white in a figure of eight works quite well.)

4 Turn into a soup tureen or individual bowls, garnish with the coriander and spring onions and serve at once.

SERVES 4

PREPARATION TIME: 10 MINUTES

COOKING TIME: 8 MINUTES

This is a colourful but easy soup to assemble. If you use vegetarian stock, you can turn this into a delectable vegetarian treat to share with friends and family.

tomato eggflower soup with beancurd

225g (8 oz) fresh or tinned whole tomatoes

225g (8 oz) soft or firm beancurd (see page 10)

1 egg

2 teaspoons sesame oil

1.2 litres (2 pints) home-made chicken or vegetarian stock (see pages 23–6) or quality store-bought fresh stock

1 teaspoon sugar

1 teaspoon salt

1 tablespoon light soy sauce

3 tablespoons finely chopped spring onions, white part only

GARNISH

3 tablespoons finely chopped spring onions, green part only

1 If you are using fresh tomatoes, peel, deseed and cut them into 2.5cm (1 in) cubes. If you are using tinned tomatoes, chop them into small chunks. Carefully cut the beancurd into small chunks as well. In a small bowl, lightly beat the egg and then combine with the sesame oil.

2 Put the stock into a wok and bring it to simmering point. Add the sugar, salt and soy sauce, and stir to mix well. Then add the beancurd and simmer for 4 minutes.

3 Next add the tomatoes and simmer for 2 minutes. Stir in the spring onions.

4 Now add the egg mixture in a very slow, thin stream. Using a chopstick or fork, pull the egg gently into strands. (I find that stirring the egg in a figure of eight works quite well.)

5 Turn into a soup tureen or individual bowls, garnish with the spring onion tops and serve at once.

One of my favourite Vietnamese dishes is Pho – a slowly cooked beef and rice noodle soup that is substantial and satisfying. Here is a much faster version that makes a warming treat, perfect for cold autumn or winter nights.

Vietnamese pho soup

225g (8 oz) minced beef
175g (6 oz) thin dried rice noodles
1.2 litres (2 pints) home-made chicken stock
   (see page 23) or quality store-bought
   fresh stock
3 whole star anise
3 whole cloves
1 cinnamon stick
2 teaspoons fish sauce or light soy sauce
1 teaspoon chilli bean sauce
2 teaspoons sugar
freshly ground white or black pepper, to
   taste

MARINADE
1 tablespoon dark soy sauce
2 teaspoons Shaoxing rice wine or dry sherry
1 teaspoon sugar
1 teaspoon sesame oil
1 teaspoon cornflour

GARNISH
4 tablespoons coarsely chopped spring
   onions
handful coarsely chopped basil leaves
handful coarsely chopped fresh coriander

1 In a medium-sized bowl, combine the marinade ingredients. Add the beef, mix well and marinate for 20 minutes in the refrigerator. Drain, discarding the marinade.

2 While the beef is marinating, soak the rice noodles in hot water for 20 minutes. When soft, drain well in a colander and set aside. Discard the water.

3 Put the stock in a wok and bring to simmering point. Add the star anise, cloves and cinnamon and simmer for 3 minutes.

4 Add the beef and stir for 1 minute, breaking up any clumps of meat.

5 Now add the fish sauce or light soy sauce, chilli bean sauce, sugar and pepper. Simmer for 2 minutes.

6 Add the rice noodles and cook for another 3 minutes.

7 Using a slotted spoon, remove the star anise, cloves and cinnamon. Turn the soup into a tureen or individual bowls, garnish with spring onions, basil and coriander and serve at once.

For centuries, Chinese vegetarians have cleverly used textures similar to meat or fish in their vegetarian dishes. Beanthread noodles, which have a toothsome bite and are rather long and chewy, provide the illusion of the similarly chewy and, on its own, rather tasteless shark's fin in this soup.

vegetarian 'shark's fin' soup

50g (2 oz) beanthread (transparent) noodles

1.2 litres (2 pints) home-made vegetarian stock (see page 24) or quality store-bought fresh stock

1 tablespoon light soy sauce

2 tablespoons dark soy sauce

1 tablespoon Shaoxing rice wine or dry sherry

2 teaspoons sugar

salt and freshly ground black pepper, to taste

2 teaspoons cornflour, mixed with 1 tablespoon cold water

2 teaspoons sesame oil

1 Soak the noodles in hot water for 15 minutes. When soft, drain well and discard the water. Cut into 7.5cm (3 in) lengths, using scissors or a knife. Set aside.

2 Heat the stock in a wok to boiling point. Turn the heat down and add the noodles, soy sauces, rice wine or sherry, sugar, salt and pepper. Gently simmer for about 4 minutes.

3 Then add the cornflour mixture and continue to cook, stirring constantly, for another 3 minutes or until the soup has slightly thickened.

4 Finally add the sesame oil and give the soup several good stirs.

5 Turn into a soup tureen or individual bowls and serve at once.

fish and shellfish

SERVES 4–6

PREPARATION TIME: 5 MINUTES

COOKING TIME: 7 MINUTES

I am delighted that mussels have come back into fashion. They are economical and quick to cook. All they need in the way of preparation is a quick scrub under cold running water to remove all the sand. I love the way they are out of the pan and on the table in minutes. Make in double quantities for larger gatherings.

mussels with ginger and spring onions

1½ tablespoons groundnut (peanut) oil

3 tablespoons coarsely chopped garlic

2 tablespoons finely shredded fresh ginger

3 tablespoons coarsely chopped spring onions

1.4kg (3 lb) fresh mussels, well scrubbed and beards removed

2 tablespoons light soy sauce

3 tablespoons water

GARNISH

handful fresh coriander sprigs

1 Heat a wok over high heat until it is hot. Add the oil, and when it is very hot and slightly smoking, add the garlic, ginger and spring onions. Stir-fry for 20 seconds.

2 Add the mussels and stir-fry for 1 minute.

3 Now add the soy sauce and water. Cover and continue to cook for 5 minutes or until all the mussels have opened. Discard any that have not opened.

4 Give the mixture a final stir before turning into a soup tureen or individual bowls. Garnish with the coriander and serve at once.

SERVES 4
PREPARATION TIME: 5 MINUTES
COOKING TIME: 6 MINUTES

Prawns are perhaps one of the easiest foods to cook and, fortunately, they are also one of the most popular. Who can resist succulent, tasty prawns? Not many of us. This recipe uses olive oil, mixing Eastern and Western ingredients for a fresh taste – a technique known as fusion cooking.

garlic prawns

450g (1 lb) raw unpeeled prawns,
   fresh or frozen
2 tablespoons extra-virgin olive oil
3 tablespoons finely sliced garlic
125g (4 oz) sliced onions
salt and freshly ground black pepper, to taste
2 teaspoons sugar

1 If using frozen prawns, defrost thoroughly. Peel the prawns and discard the shells. Using a small sharp knife, remove the fine digestive cord. Wash them, drain and pat dry with kitchen paper.

2 Heat a wok over high heat until it is hot. Add the oil, and when it is hot and slightly smoking, add the garlic and onions. Stir-fry for 2 minutes or until golden brown.

3 Then add the prawns, salt, pepper and sugar, and stir-fry for about 4 minutes or until the prawns are pink.

4 Turn onto a warm platter and serve at once.

Stir-frying prawns is perhaps one of the simplest ways to make a quick but elegant meal. Prawns are everyone's favourite. For convenience, this recipe uses ordinary chives, rather than the more usual traditional Chinese chives.

stir-fried prawns with chives

450g (1 lb) raw unpeeled prawns, fresh or frozen

2 tablespoons groundnut (peanut) oil

225g (8 oz) thickly sliced onions

1 teaspoon salt

freshly ground white pepper, to taste

2 teaspoons sesame oil

6 tablespoons chives, cut in 2.5cm (1 in) segments

MARINADE

1 teaspoon sesame oil

salt and freshly ground black pepper, to taste

P Can be prepared ahead: cover the prawns and refrigerate for up to 2 hours.

1 If using frozen prawns, defrost thoroughly. Peel the prawns, discarding the shells. Using a small, sharp knife, remove the fine digestive cord. Wash them, drain and pat dry with kitchen paper.

2 In a medium-sized bowl, combine the marinade ingredients. Add the prawns, mix well and marinate for 15 minutes in the refrigerator. Drain, discarding the marinade. P

3 Heat a wok over high heat until it is hot and then add the oil. When the oil is very hot and slightly smoking, add the onions and stir-fry for 3–4 minutes or until golden brown.

4 Add the prawns, together with the salt and pepper. Stir-fry for 4 minutes or until the prawns turn pink.

5 Stir in the sesame oil, give the mixture a couple of good stirs and continue to stir-fry for another 3 minutes.

6 Finally add the chives and continue to stir-fry for 1 further minute or until the chives have wilted.

7 Turn onto a warm platter and serve at once.

fish and shellfish 59

I like to serve this quick and easy prawn dish with Five-Spice Chips (see page 124) and a salad, although they are perfect just with lemon wedges. You will need to cook the prawns in batches to make sure they are cooked properly and crisply.

crispy prawns

450g (1 lb) raw unpeeled prawns, fresh or
  frozen
450ml (14 fl oz) groundnut (peanut) oil

BATTER
50g (2 oz) cornflour
25g (1 oz) plain flour
1 teaspoon baking powder
1 teaspoon chilli powder (optional)
1 teaspoon Madras curry powder
salt and freshly ground black pepper, to taste
1 teaspoon sesame oil
85ml (3 fl oz) water

TO SERVE
lemon wedges

1 If using frozen prawns, defrost thoroughly. Peel the prawns and discard the shells. Using a small sharp knife, remove the fine digestive cord. Wash them, drain and pat dry with kitchen paper.

2 In a medium-sized bowl, combine the batter ingredients. Whisk together until smooth. Stir the prawns into the batter to coat them.

3 Heat a wok over high heat until it is hot and swirl in the groundnut oil. When it is very hot and slightly smoking, turn the heat down to moderate. Lift the prawns from the batter with a slotted spoon and deep-fry in several batches until pink. Remove each batch when it is cooked and place on a tray lined with kitchen paper to drain. Repeat with the remaining prawns.

4 When all the prawns are cooked, turn onto a warm platter and serve at once with the lemon wedges.

SERVES 4

PREPARATION TIME: 5 MINUTES

COOKING TIME: 15 MINUTES

Steaming is probably one of the healthiest and best cooking techniques for delicate scallops. They are gently poached in the hot vapours without getting overcooked. With Chinese black beans, they become a special savoury treat. The bonus is that this recipe is fast and easy.

steamed scallops with black beans

450g (1 lb) fresh scallops, including the corals
2 tablespoons chopped black beans
2 tablespoons coarsely chopped garlic
2 teaspoons finely chopped fresh ginger
1 tablespoon Shaoxing rice wine or dry sherry
1 tablespoon light soy sauce
salt and freshly ground black pepper, to taste

GARNISH
handful fresh coriander sprigs

1 Remove the hard muscle from each scallop and discard. Distribute the scallops evenly on a heatproof platter. In a small bowl, combine the black beans, garlic, ginger, rice wine or sherry, soy sauce, salt and pepper. Sprinkle evenly over the scallops.

2 Next set up a steamer or put a rack into a wok and fill it with 5cm (2 in) of water. Bring the water to the boil over a high heat. Carefully lower the scallops into the steamer or onto the rack. Turn the heat to low and cover the wok tightly. Steam gently for 12–15 minutes, depending on the size of the scallops. They should feel firm to the touch when cooked.

3 Turn onto a warm platter, garnish with the coriander and serve at once.

Although the combination of prawns and cucumber may sound unusual, it is a surprisingly delicious match. Both of the main ingredients are ideal for fast wok cooking.

stir-fried prawns with cucumber

450g (1 lb) cucumbers (about 1)

2 teaspoons salt

450g (1 lb) raw, unpeeled prawns, fresh or frozen

2 tablespoons groundnut (peanut) oil

3 tablespoons coarsely chopped garlic

2 teaspoons finely chopped fresh ginger

salt and freshly ground black pepper, to taste

2 teaspoons sesame oil

MARINADE

1 teaspoon sesame oil

salt and freshly ground white pepper, to taste

1 Peel the cucumbers, slice in half lengthways and, using a teaspoon, remove the seeds. Then cut into 2.5cm (1 in) cubes. Sprinkle them with the salt and combine thoroughly. Put into a colander and leave to stand for 20 minutes to drain. This gets rid of any excess liquid.

2 While they are draining, prepare the prawns. If using frozen prawns, defrost thoroughly. Peel, and discard the shells. Using a small, sharp knife, remove the fine digestive cord. Wash them, drain and pat dry with kitchen paper. In a large bowl, combine the marinade ingredients. Add the prawns, mix well and marinate for 15 minutes in the refrigerator. Drain, discarding the marinade.

3 When the cucumber has drained for 20 minutes, rinse thoroughly in cold water and blot dry with kitchen paper.

4 Heat a wok over high heat until it is hot and then add the oil. When the oil is very hot and slightly smoking, add the garlic, ginger and cucumber and stir-fry for 3 minutes.

5 Add the prawns, salt and pepper, and stir-fry for 4 minutes or until the prawns turn pink.

6 Then stir in the sesame oil, give the mixture a couple of good stirs and leave to cook undisturbed for another 3 minutes.

7 Turn onto a warm platter and serve at once.

SERVES 4
PREPARATION TIME: 20 MINUTES
COOKING TIME: 8 MINUTES

Prawns are perfect for a fast but tasty meal. Succulent and irresistible, they are always popular and no wonder. They pair easily with other flavours, as here with coriander and orange. This sounds an unlikely combination, but is absolutely delicious.

stir-fried coriander and orange prawns

450g (1 lb) raw, unpeeled prawns,
    fresh or frozen
1 tablespoon groundnut (peanut) oil
1 tablespoon extra-virgin olive oil
salt and freshly ground white pepper, to
    taste
2 tablespoons finely chopped orange zest
2 teaspoons sesame oil
3 tablespoons finely chopped fresh
    coriander

MARINADE
1 teaspoon sesame oil
salt and freshly ground black pepper, to taste

1 If using frozen prawns, defrost thoroughly. Peel the prawns and discard the shells. Using a small, sharp knife, remove the fine digestive cord. Wash them, drain and pat dry with kitchen paper. In a large bowl, combine the marinade ingredients. Add the prawns, mix well and marinate for 15 minutes in the refrigerator. Drain, discarding the marinade.

2 Heat a wok over high heat until it is very hot and then add the groundnut and olive oils. When they are very hot and slightly smoking, add the prawns, together with the salt, pepper and orange zest, and stir-fry for 4 minutes or until the prawns turn pink.

3 Stir in the sesame oil, give the mixture a couple of good stirs and continue to stir-fry for another 3 minutes.

4 Finally add the coriander and continue to stir-fry for 1 further minute.

5 Turn onto a warm platter and serve at once.

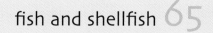

Fresh fish is perhaps one of the healthiest foods that can be cooked quickly in a wok. Here the fish is served with a simple tomato sauce that is just as quick to make. Olive oil is the perfect complement to tomatoes.

pan-fried fish in spicy tomato sauce

450g (1 lb) boneless, firm white fish fillets, such as cod, sea bass or halibut, skinned and divided into 4 equal pieces
salt and freshly ground black pepper, to taste
plain flour, for dusting
450g (1 lb) tinned whole tomatoes
3 tablespoons extra-virgin olive oil
3 tablespoons coarsely chopped garlic
2 tablespoons finely chopped shallots
1 tablespoon Shaoxing rice wine or dry sherry
1 tablespoon light soy sauce
1 tablespoon chilli bean sauce
2 teaspoons sugar

GARNISH
handful fresh basil leaves

1 Pat the fish dry with kitchen paper. Sprinkle evenly with the salt and pepper and dust with flour, shaking off any excess. Drain the tomatoes, reserving the juice, and chop the flesh into small chunks. Measure the amount of juice, keep half and set aside. Discard the rest.

2 Heat a wok over high heat until it is hot. Add the olive oil, and when it is moderately hot, add the fish fillets and pan-fry them for 3–5 minutes, depending on the thickness of the fillets. Then turn them over and brown the other side (this will also take about 3–5 minutes). When cooked, remove and drain on kitchen paper. Turn onto a warm platter.

3 Now make the sauce. Pour off all but 1 tablespoon of oil from the wok, add the garlic and shallots, and stir-fry for 1 minute.

4 Add the tomatoes, the reserved tomato juice, rice wine or sherry, soy sauce, chilli bean sauce and sugar, and simmer for 5 minutes.

5 Pour the sauce over the fish, garnish with the basil and serve at once.

Steaming fish is not only healthy but fast. In this easy recipe, the gentle vapours preserve the subtle taste of the fish and keep it moist. Ginger plays the same role in Eastern fish cookery as lemon does in the West, balancing the fishy flavours.

steamed ginger fish

450g (1 lb) boneless, firm white fish fillets, such as cod or plaice, skinned and divided into 4 equal pieces, or a whole fish such as sole, sea bass or turbot
Maldon sea salt or ordinary salt, to taste
2 tablespoons finely shredded fresh ginger
1 tablespoon orange zest
1 tablespoon lemon zest
3 tablespoons finely shredded spring onions
handful fresh basil leaves
2 tablespoons light soy sauce
1 tablespoon groundnut (peanut) oil
1 tablespoon extra-virgin olive oil

1 Pat dry the fish or fish fillets with kitchen paper and rub salt evenly over both sides. Place on a heatproof plate and scatter the ginger, orange and lemon zest evenly over the top.

2 Next set up a steamer or put a rack into a wok and fill it with 5cm (2 in) of water. Bring the water to the boil over a high heat. Put the plate of fish into the steamer or onto the rack. Cover the pan tightly and gently steam the fish until it is just cooked. Flat fish will take about 5 minutes to cook. Whole fish or thicker fillets such as cod or sea bass will take 12–14 minutes. The fish is cooked when it turns opaque and flakes slightly but still remains moist.

3 When cooked, remove the fish, pouring off any excess liquid that may have accumulated. Arrange on a warm platter. Sprinkle with the spring onions, basil and soy sauce.

4 To complete the dish, heat the two oils together in a small saucepan until they are smoking. When hot, pour over the fish and serve at once.

SERVES 4

PREPARATION TIME: 25 MINUTES

COOKING TIME: 10 MINUTES

This is a luscious but simple combination that really works. Not only is it quick to cook but it makes a fabulous main course for an impromptu dinner party.

stir-fried fish and spinach

450g (1 lb) boneless, firm white fish fillets, such as cod, halibut or sea bass, skinned and divided into 4 equal pieces
2 teaspoons salt
675g (1½ lb) fresh spinach
4 tablespoons groundnut (peanut) oil
2 tablespoons coarsely chopped garlic
1 teaspoon caster sugar
2 teaspoons sesame oil

P Can be prepared ahead: cover the fish and refrigerate for up to 2 hours; cover the spinach and refrigerate for up to 6 hours.

1 Pat the fish dry with kitchen paper. Cut into strips 2.5cm (1 in) wide. Lay in a dish and sprinkle evenly with the salt. Refrigerate for 20 minutes.

2 Wash the spinach thoroughly in at least two changes of water. Drain thoroughly in a colander. Remove all the stems, retaining just the leaves. **P**

3 Heat a wok over high heat until it is hot. Add 3 tablespoons of the groundnut oil, and when it is very hot and slightly smoking, turn the heat down to medium and add the fish strips. Let them pan-fry undisturbed for about 2 minutes. Then gently turn them over to brown on the other side for about 2 minutes. Take care not to break them up. Remove with a fish slice and drain on kitchen paper.

4 Reheat the wok over high heat and add the remaining groundnut oil. Add the garlic and a little salt, and stir-fry for 20 seconds to brown. Now add the spinach, one half at a time. Stir-fry for about 2 minutes to coat the spinach leaves thoroughly with the oil, garlic and salt.

5 When the spinach has wilted to about one-third of its original size, add the sugar and continue to stir-fry for another 2 minutes.

6 Return the fish to the wok, and gently combine with the spinach for about 1 minute. Then add the sesame oil and give the mixture a good stir.

7 Using a slotted spoon or fish slice, turn onto a warm serving platter and serve at once.

Steaming oysters keeps them succulent and prevents them from drying out. Also steaming is a healthy and quick way to cook. If you don't have an oyster knife, an ordinary knife will do. And don't worry if you can't open the oysters; once they have been steamed, they will usually open automatically.

steamed oysters with ginger sauce

16 large fresh oysters

SAUCE
4 tablespoons finely chopped spring
    onions, white part only
2 teaspoons finely chopped fresh ginger
salt and freshly ground black pepper, to taste
2 teaspoons sesame oil

GARNISH
handful fresh coriander sprigs

1 Scrub the oysters clean. Open them with an oyster knife. Divide them into two batches and place on two heatproof plates; this is because you will have to steam each batch separately.

2 Next set up a steamer or put a rack into a wok and fill it with 5cm (2 in) of water. Bring the water to the boil over a high heat. Put one batch of oysters on their plate into the steamer or onto the rack. Turn the heat down to low and cover the wok tightly. Steam gently for 5–6 minutes.

3 While they are cooking, combine all the sauce ingredients in a bowl and stir well.

4 Remove the first batch of oysters from the steamer and turn onto a warm platter. Pour a little sauce over each cooked oyster, reserving half the sauce for the second batch. Garnish with coriander and serve immediately.

5 Repeat steps 2–4 for the second batch.

Fresh tuna, simply seared in a hot wok, has become very popular, and it is ideal for fast cooking. Just remember two things: if overcooked, tuna can quickly dry out, and it is important to get the highest quality tuna you can afford.

spicy tuna

4 fresh tuna steaks, about 100g (4 oz) each, cut thickly
3 tablespoons extra-virgin olive oil

SPICE MIX
1 teaspoon chilli powder (optional)
1 teaspoon Madras curry powder
1 teaspoon sugar
salt and freshly ground black pepper, to taste

GARNISH
handful fresh coriander sprigs

1 Lay the tuna steaks on a platter. In a small bowl, combine the ingredients for the spice mix and blend thoroughly. Sprinkle this evenly over both sides of the tuna steaks.

2 Heat a wok over high heat and when it is hot, add the oil. When the oil is very hot and slightly smoking, add the tuna steaks and sear them on one side for 2 minutes.

3 Turn them over and sear the other side for 2 minutes. The tuna should remain 'rare'.

4 Turn them onto a warm platter, garnish with the coriander and serve at once.

poultry

This is a delicious variation on a popular dish from one of my restaurants. The first part of the recipe can be completed a few hours ahead: refrigerate the chicken when it has been oven-baked (at the end of stage 3), and add 3–4 minutes to the cooking time at stage 8 to ensure that it is heated through.

sweet ginger chicken

450g (1 lb) boneless, skinless chicken thighs

1 tablespoon groundnut (peanut) oil

2 teaspoons sesame oil

3 tablespoons coarsely chopped fresh ginger

2 tablespoons dark soy sauce

2 tablespoons sugar

salt and freshly ground black pepper, to taste

150ml (5 fl oz) home-made chicken stock (see page 23) or quality store-bought fresh stock

2 tablespoons Shaoxing rice wine or dry sherry

MARINADE

2 teaspoons light soy sauce

1 teaspoon dark soy sauce

1 tablespoon Shaoxing rice wine or dry sherry

salt and freshly ground black pepper, to taste

1 teaspoon sesame oil

2 teaspoons cornflour

GARNISH

3 tablespoons finely shredded spring onions

1 Cut the chicken into 5cm (2 in) chunks and place in a large bowl. In a medium-sized bowl, combine the ingredients for the marinade. Pour over the chicken and stir well to ensure all the pieces are thoroughly coated. Marinate for about 30 minutes at room temperature. Drain, discarding the marinade. Place the chicken pieces on a large baking tray.

2 Preheat the oven to 240°C, 475°F, gas mark 9.

3 In a small bowl, combine the groundnut and sesame oils. Pour over the chicken pieces and cook in the oven for 15 minutes or until golden brown. Remove with a slotted spoon, drain off all the fat and rest on kitchen paper.

4 Now heat a wok over high heat until it is hot. Add the ginger and stir-fry in the dry wok until it is crispy; this will take about 1 minute.

5 Then add the soy sauce, sugar, salt, pepper and stock, and continue to stir-fry for 1 minute. Reduce the heat, cover the wok and simmer for 8 minutes.

6 Remove the lid, turn the heat up to high and reduce the sauce by about half, stirring occasionally.

7 When the sauce has been reduced, add the rice wine or sherry and continue to stir-fry for 2 minutes.

8 Now add the chicken and stir-fry for 3–4 minutes or until it is hot.

9 Turn onto a warm platter, garnish with the spring onions and serve at once.

Chicken fried in a crispy batter is always a great favourite. It is even tastier with this mouth-watering spring onion and ginger sauce that is easy to make. The marinating can be done a few hours in advance, as can the preparation of the sauce and the batter. If preparing ahead, keep refrigerated for up to 4 hours.

chicken with onion and ginger sauce

450g (1 lb) boneless, skinless chicken thighs
450ml (14 fl oz) groundnut (peanut) oil

MARINADE
salt and freshly ground black pepper, to taste
1 teaspoon sesame oil
1 teaspoon light soy sauce
1 teaspoon Shaoxing rice wine or dry sherry
1 teaspoon cornflour

SAUCE
4 tablespoons finely chopped spring
  onions, white part only
2 teaspoons finely chopped fresh ginger
salt, to taste
2 tablespoons groundnut (peanut) oil

BATTER
50g (2 oz) cornflour
25g (1 oz) plain flour
1 teaspoon baking powder
1 teaspoon bicarbonate of soda
salt and freshly ground black pepper, to taste
1 teaspoon groundnut (peanut) oil
85ml (3 fl oz) water

1 Cut the chicken into 2.5cm (1 in) pieces. In a medium-sized bowl, combine the marinade ingredients. Add the chicken, mix well to ensure that the pieces are evenly coated and marinate for 30 minutes in the refrigerator. Drain, discarding the marinade. Set aside.

2 While the chicken is marinating, make the sauce. In a small bowl, combine the spring onions, ginger and salt, and mix well.

3 Next, make the batter. In a medium-sized bowl, combine the batter ingredients with a whisk and beat until smooth. Stir in the chicken to coat thoroughly. Remove the pieces with a slotted spoon.

4 Heat a wok over high heat until it is hot, then add the 2 tablespoons of groundnut oil for the sauce. When it is very hot and slightly smoking, pour into the bowl with the sauce ingredients and mix well.

5 Reheat the wok over high heat until it is hot and then swirl in the 450ml (14 fl oz) of groundnut oil. When it is very hot and slightly smoking, turn the heat down. Deep-fry the chicken pieces in several batches until golden brown. When cooked, drain each batch on a tray lined with kitchen paper.

6 When all the chicken pieces have been deep-fried, turn onto a warm platter, garnish with a few sliced spring onions if you like and serve with the sauce.

Whole duck breasts can now be found in supermarkets and are ideal for fast cooking, especially in the wok. Since they are tender and do not need much cooking, I think they should ideally be served like a lean piece of beef – slightly rare. This dish is impressive without needing much work or fuss.

savoury duck with oyster sauce

450g (1 lb) boneless, skinless duck breasts
3 tablespoons groundnut (peanut) oil
3 tablespoons coarsely chopped garlic
225g (8 oz) sliced onions
3 tablespoons oyster sauce
1 tablespoon Shaoxing rice wine or dry sherry
1 teaspoon sugar
handful fresh coriander sprigs

MARINADE
2 teaspoons light soy sauce
2 teaspoons Shaoxing rice wine or dry sherry
2 teaspoons sesame oil
salt and freshly ground black pepper, to taste
2 teaspoons cornflour

1 Cut the duck breasts into thick slices 4 x 1cm (1½ x ½ in). In a medium-sized bowl, combine the marinade ingredients. Add the duck, mix well and marinate for about 15 minutes at room temperature. Drain, discarding the marinade.

2 Heat a wok over high heat until it is very hot. Add the oil, and when it is very hot and slightly smoking, add the duck and stir-fry for about 2 minutes. When cooked, the duck should be slightly pink. Remove and drain in a colander.

3 Pour off all but 1½ tablespoons of the oil and reheat the wok over high heat. When it is hot, add the garlic and onion and stir-fry for 3 minutes or until the onions are brown and soft.

4 Turn the heat down to low and add the oyster sauce, rice wine or sherry and sugar, and stir for 2 minutes.

5 Return the duck to the wok. Stir to mix well and toss in the coriander.

6 Turn onto a warm platter and serve at once.

SERVES 4

PREPARATION TIME: 5 MINUTES

COOKING TIME: 8 MINUTES

Nothing is quicker or simpler than chicken stir-fried in a hot wok. The heat sears the chicken and gives it a lovely smoky flavour as well. Here aromatic basil adds an extra tang. All wok cookery is fast, but for speed this recipe takes some beating.

chicken with basil

450g (1 lb) boneless, skinless chicken breasts
1½ tablespoons groundnut (peanut) oil
3 tablespoons coarsely chopped garlic
1 teaspoon finely chopped fresh ginger
50ml (2 fl oz) home-made chicken stock (see page 23) or quality store-bought fresh stock
1 tablespoon light soy sauce
2 teaspoons sugar
2 teaspoons chilli bean sauce
2 teaspoons sesame oil
handful fresh basil leaves

1 Cut the chicken into long strips about 4 x 1cm (1½ x ½ in).

2 Heat a wok over high heat until it is hot, then add the oil. When it is hot, add the garlic and ginger and stir-fry for 20 seconds.

3 Then add the chicken and stir-fry for 2 minutes.

4 Add the stock, soy sauce, sugar and chilli bean sauce, and stir well. Bring to simmering point and simmer for 5 minutes.

5 Finally, stir in the sesame oil and toss in the basil, mixing well.

6 Turn onto a warm platter and serve at once.

This is a fast version of a Hong Kong-inspired dish. Each guest places a portion of the chicken in a lettuce leaf, wraps the leaf around it and eats with their fingers. Delicious finger food and tremendous fun for an informal party.

chicken in lettuce cups

275g (1 lb) boneless, skinless chicken breasts

1½ tablespoons groundnut (peanut) oil

2 tablespoons coarsely chopped garlic

50g (2 oz) cashew nuts, coarsely chopped

50g (2 oz) tinned smoked oysters, finely chopped

2 tablespoons coarsely chopped cooked ham

1 tablespoon finely chopped fresh ginger

3 tablespoons finely chopped fresh coriander

50g (2 oz) tinned bamboo shoots, finely chopped

50g (2 oz) fresh or tinned water chestnuts, finely chopped

3 tablespoons finely chopped spring onions

5 tablespoons oyster sauce

2 teaspoons sugar

salt and freshly ground black pepper, to taste

TO SERVE

225g (8 oz) iceberg lettuce, separated into leaves

1 Prepare the vegetables. Dice the chicken into small 5mm (¼ in) cubes.

2 Heat a wok over a high heat until it is hot. Add the oil, and when it is very hot and slightly smoking, add the garlic and stir-fry for 20 seconds. Then add the chicken and stir-fry for 1 further minute.

3 Next, add the cashew nuts, oysters, ham, ginger, coriander, bamboo shoots, water chestnuts and spring onions, and continue to sir-fry for 3 minutes.

4 Finally, add the oyster sauce, sugar, salt and pepper, and continue to stir-fry for 3 minutes.

5 Turn onto a warm platter and serve at once, accompanied by the lettuce leaves arranged on a separate platter.

Unlike most curries, this delectable Thai-style version is put together in a matter of minutes. It is also very easy.

Thai-style chicken curry

450g (1 lb) boneless, skinless chicken breasts

400ml (14 fl oz) tin coconut milk

1–2 tablespoons red Thai curry paste, to taste

3 tablespoons finely shredded spring onions

1½ tablespoons finely shredded fresh ginger

1½ tablespoons Shaoxing rice wine or dry sherry

1 tablespoon fish sauce or light soy sauce

1 teaspoon lime juice

salt and freshly ground black pepper, to taste

2 teaspoons sugar

GARNISH

handful fresh coriander sprigs

1 Cut the chicken into 2.5cm (1 in) cubes.

2 In a wok, combine the coconut milk, curry paste, spring onions, ginger, rice wine or sherry, fish sauce or soy sauce, lime juice, salt, pepper and sugar. Bring to simmering point.

3 Add the chicken. Immediately cover the wok tightly, remove it from the heat and stand, covered, for 15 minutes, to allow the chicken to steep in the hot curry sauce.

4 Turn onto a warm platter, garnish with the coriander and serve at once.

This is a high-speed dish that comes together in minutes. Much of the work – the marinating and the sauce – can be done in advance: covered and refrigerated, the chicken can be kept for up to 4 hours and the sauce for up to 24. It is ideal for last-minute entertaining as well.

chicken with satay sauce

450g (1 lb) boneless, skinless chicken breasts
1½ tablespoons groundnut (peanut) oil

MARINADE
3 tablespoons light soy sauce
1 tablespoon Shaoxing rice wine or dry sherry
salt and freshly ground black pepper, to taste
2 teaspoons cornflour

SAUCE
3 tablespoons sesame paste or smooth
  peanut butter
1 tablespoon chilli bean sauce
1 tablespoon coarsely chopped garlic
2 teaspoons chilli oil
2 tablespoons Chinese white rice vinegar or
  cider vinegar
2 tablespoons light soy sauce
salt and freshly ground black pepper, to taste
2 teaspoons sugar
2 tablespoons hot water

GARNISH
50g (2oz) thinly sliced onions
100g (4 oz) thinly sliced cucumbers

1 Cut the chicken into 2.5cm (1 in) cubes. In a medium-sized bowl, combine the marinade ingredients. Add the chicken, mix well and leave to marinate for at least 20 minutes at room temperature. Drain, discarding the marinade.

2 Put all the ingredients for the sauce in a blender or food processor and process until smooth.

3 Heat a wok over high heat until it is very hot, then add the oil. When the oil is very hot and slightly smoking, add the chicken and stir-fry for 5 minutes.

4 Turn the heat down to low, add the sauce and continue to stir-fry for another 5 minutes.

5 Turn onto a warm platter, garnish with the onion and cucumber and serve at once.

SERVES 4

PREPARATION TIME: 5 MINUTES

COOKING TIME: 12 MINUTES

Chef Ban Yun Long of the Chinese Embassy in London is the inspiration behind this delicious recipe. If you don't like dishes to be too spicy, substitute milder red chillies. And if you can't find chicken ready-minced, you can either mince it in a food processor or chop it with a cleaver – which takes no time at all.

tasty chicken with mushrooms

450g (1 lb) button mushrooms

1 tablespoon groundnut (peanut) oil

1 tablespoon sesame oil

2 tablespoons coarsely chopped garlic

2 fresh green chillies, seeded and shredded

1 tablespoon Shaoxing rice wine or dry sherry

salt and freshly ground black pepper, to taste

2 teaspoons sugar

225g (8 oz) boneless, skinless chicken breasts, minced

3 tablespoons finely chopped spring onions

1 Wipe the mushrooms with a damp cloth and slice finely.

2 Heat a wok over a high heat until it is hot. Add the groundnut and sesame oils, and when they are very hot and slightly smoking, add the garlic and chillies. Stir-fry for about 20 seconds.

3 Add the mushrooms and stir-fry for about 3 minutes.

4 Add the rice wine or sherry, salt, pepper and sugar, and continue to stir-fry for about 5 minutes or until the mushrooms are cooked through and have absorbed any excess liquid.

5 Now add the chicken and stir-fry for 4 minutes.

6 Just before serving, add the spring onions and give the mixture a couple of good stirs.

7 Turn onto a warm platter and serve at once.

Chicken livers are among the easiest and most inexpensive foods to prepare. They are especially delicious when quickly stir-fried in a hot wok.

spicy chicken livers

450g (1 lb) chicken livers

1 tablespoon Shaoxing rice wine or dry sherry

1 tablespoon light soy sauce

3 teaspoons sesame oil

salt and freshly ground black pepper, to taste

1 tablespoon cornflour

2 tablespoons groundnut (peanut) oil

SAUCE

1 tablespoon chilli bean sauce

2 tablespoons hoisin sauce

2 teaspoons oyster sauce

1 tablespoon Shaoxing rice wine or dry sherry

1 Cut the chicken livers into bite-sized pieces. In a medium-sized bowl, combine the rice wine or sherry, soy sauce, 1 teaspoon of the sesame oil, salt, pepper and cornflour. Add the livers and mix well to coat thoroughly.

2 Heat a wok over high heat until it is very hot, then add the oil. When it is hot, add the livers and let them brown undisturbed for 2 minutes.

3 Then turn them over and let them brown on the other side for another 2 minutes. When cooked, they should still be pink inside. Remove with a slotted spoon and drain on kitchen paper.

4 In a small bowl, combine the ingredients for the sauce.

5 Pour off any excess oil from the wok and wipe it clean with kitchen paper. Reheat the wok over high heat and when it is hot, pour in the sauce. When this is hot, return the livers to the wok, drizzle in the remaining sesame oil and stir-fry for 2 more minutes.

6 Turn onto a warm platter and serve at once.

meat

Stir-frying is a fast and different way to cook lamb. Here it is combined with two aromatic ingredients – garlic and basil – for an unusual but delicious dish.

stir-fried lamb with garlic and basil

450g (1 lb) lean lamb steaks or fillets or
  boned loin chops
2 tablespoons groundnut (peanut) oil
6 garlic cloves, peeled and thinly sliced
salt and freshly ground black pepper, to taste
handful fresh basil leaves
handful fresh coriander sprigs

MARINADE
1 tablespoon Shaoxing rice wine or dry
  sherry
1 tablespoon light soy sauce
2 teaspoons sesame oil
2 teaspoons cornflour

1 Cut the lamb into thin slices. In a medium-sized bowl, combine the ingredients for the marinade. Add the lamb, mix well and marinate for 20 minutes at room temperature. Drain, discarding the marinade.

2 Heat a wok over high heat until it is very hot. Add the oil, and when it is very hot and slightly smoking, add the lamb and stir-fry for 2 minutes.

3 Add the garlic, salt and pepper, and continue to stir-fry for another 3 minutes.

4 Finally toss in the basil and coriander, and continue to stir-fry for 1 further minute or until the herbs have wilted.

5 Turn onto a warm serving platter and serve at once.

Unlike most curries, this delicious lamb curry is quick to make. It goes well with plain steamed rice.

Thai-style lamb curry

225g (8 oz) potatoes

225g (8 oz) carrots

1 tablespoon groundnut (peanut) oil

1–2 tablespoons Thai green curry paste, to taste

400ml (14 fl oz) tin coconut milk

3 tablespoons fish sauce or light soy sauce

salt, to taste

2 teaspoons lime zest

2 teaspoons sugar

300ml (10 fl oz) home-made chicken stock (see page 23) or quality store-bought fresh stock

450g (1 lb) minced lamb

handful fresh basil leaves

1 Peel the potatoes and cut into 2.5cm (1 in) cubes. Peel the carrots and roll-cut them (see page 21) into 2.5cm (1 in) lengths.

2 Heat a wok over high heat until it is hot. Add the oil, and when it is very hot and slightly smoking, add the curry paste and stir-fry for 20 seconds.

3 Slowly drizzle in the coconut milk, stirring continuously until blended. Then add the fish sauce or soy sauce, salt, lime zest, sugar and stock. Stir until blended.

4 Finally, add the lamb, potatoes and carrots. Turn the heat down to low, cover the pan or wok, and simmer for 15–20 minutes, or until the vegetables are tender.

5 Toss in the basil and stir to mix well.

6 Turn onto a warm platter and serve at once.

This is real fusion cooking – a marriage of East and West. I find this quick and tasty recipe so good that I often simply toss in some cooked pasta, drizzle in a little olive oil and serve it just as it is. However, it is equally good with plain steamed rice. The secret is to use minced pork, which cooks fast and absorbs more flavour.

savoury garlic pork

1½ tablespoons groundnut (peanut) oil
2 teaspoons extra-virgin olive oil
6 tablespoons coarsely chopped garlic
1 teaspoon chilli powder (optional)
450g (1 lb) minced pork
2 tablespoons finely chopped fresh parsley
salt and freshly ground black pepper, to taste
1 tablespoon light soy sauce
2 teaspoons sugar
50ml (2 fl oz) home-made chicken stock
   (see page 23) or quality store-bought
   fresh stock
handful fresh basil leaves

1 Heat a wok over high heat until it is hot. Add the two oils, and when they are very hot and slightly smoking, add the garlic and chilli powder, if using, and stir-fry for 30 seconds.

2 Add the pork and stir-fry for 3 minutes.

3 Then add the parsley, salt, pepper, soy sauce, sugar and stock, and continue to stir-fry for 3 minutes. Check that the pork is cooked through and that there is no trace of pink.

4 Finally, add the basil and stir-fry for 1 further minute.

5 Turn onto a warm platter and serve at once.

SERVES 4

PREPARATION TIME: 1 MINUTE

COOKING TIME: 7 MINUTES

This is a spicy way to combine two of my favourite foods – sweetcorn and pork – in a recipe that takes literally minutes. If you like your food 'hot', use green or hot red chillies.

firecracker pork with corn

275g (10 oz) fresh sweetcorn (about 2 ears), cooked, or frozen corn

1 tablespoon groundnut (peanut) oil

225g (8 oz) minced pork

2 small fresh red chillies, seeded and finely chopped

salt and freshly ground black pepper, to taste

1 teaspoon sugar

1 tablespoon Shaoxing rice wine or dry sherry

1 tablespoon light soy sauce

2 teaspoons sesame oil

1 If using fresh corn, cut the kernels off the cobs. If using frozen corn, blanch for 10 seconds in a pan of boiling water and drain. Set aside.

2 Heat a wok over high heat until it is hot. Add the oil, and when it is very hot and slightly smoking, add the pork and stir-fry for 3 minutes.

3 Add the corn, chillies, salt and pepper, and stir-fry for 1 minute.

4 Next, add the sugar, rice wine or sherry and soy sauce, and continue to stir-fry for 2 minutes.

5 Finally, stir in the sesame oil and mix well.

6 Turn onto a warm platter and serve at once.

Stir-frying is such a versatile and innovative way to cook. You can put together almost any combination of foods in the wok. Here pork is paired with sharp pineapple to give an almost sweet-and-sour taste to this easy-to-make dish.

pineapple pork

450g (1 lb) pork fillet

1½ tablespoons groundnut (peanut) oil

3 tablespoons coarsely chopped garlic

225g (8 oz) fresh or tinned pineapple, chopped

2 tablespoons finely chopped fresh coriander

1 tablespoon dark soy sauce

2 teaspoons sugar

MARINADE

2 teaspoons light soy sauce

2 teaspoons Shaoxing rice wine or dry sherry

1 teaspoon sesame oil

2 teaspoons cornflour

GARNISH

handful fresh coriander sprigs

1 Cut the pork into thin strips about 5cm (2 in) long. In a medium-sized bowl, combine the marinade ingredients. Add the pork, mix well and leave to marinate at room temperature while you prepare the other ingredients. Drain, discarding the marinade.

2 Heat a wok over high heat until it is hot. Add the oil, and when it is very hot and slightly smoking, add the garlic and stir-fry for 15 seconds or until golden brown.

3 Add the pork and stir-fry for 3 minutes.

4 Finally, add the pineapple, coriander, soy sauce and sugar, and continue to stir-fry for 3 minutes.

5 Turn onto a warm platter, garnish with the coriander and serve at once.

SERVES 2 AS A MAIN COURSE,
4 AS A SIDE DISH
PREPARATION TIME: 25 MINUTES
COOKING TIME: 12 MINUTES

Cucumbers are among the few vegetables to be found in virtually every fridge. Not only do they make an easy salad, but they are also a refreshing cooked vegetable when combined with meat. This fast dish requires little work and the cucumbers are half 'cooked' by the salt.

pork with cucumber

675g (1½ lb) cucumbers (about 1½)
2 teaspoons salt
1½ tablespoons groundnut (peanut) oil
3 tablespoons coarsely chopped garlic
450g (1 lb) minced pork
2 tablespoons finely chopped fresh
    coriander
2 tablespoons soy sauce
2 tablespoons oyster sauce
2 teaspoons sugar
50ml (2 fl oz) home-made chicken stock
    (see page 23) or quality store-bought
    fresh stock

GARNISH
handful fresh coriander sprigs

1 Peel the cucumbers, slice them in half lengthways and, using a teaspoon, remove the seeds. Then cut into 2.5cm (1 in) cubes. Sprinkle with the salt and mix well. Turn into a colander and stand for 20 minutes to drain. This gets rid of any excess liquid. Rinse in cold water and blot dry with kitchen paper.

2 Heat a wok over high heat until it is hot. Add the oil, and when it is very hot and slightly smoking, add the garlic and stir-fry for 30 seconds.

3 Add the pork and stir-fry for 3 minutes.

4 Next, add the coriander, soy sauce, oyster sauce, sugar and stock, and continue to stir-fry for 3 minutes.

5 Finally, add the cucumber and stir-fry for 5 minutes.

6 Turn onto a warm platter, garnish with the coriander and serve at once.

This is one of the easiest and tastiest ways to rustle up a quick meal. Pork cooks fast in the wok and the nuts add an irresistible and satisfying crunch.

stir-fried pork with cashew nuts

450g (1 lb) lean pork fillet
2 tablespoons groundnut (peanut) oil
50g (2 oz) raw cashew nuts
salt and freshly ground black pepper, to taste
1 teaspoon sugar

MARINADE
1 tablespoon Shaoxing rice wine or dry
   sherry
1 tablespoon light soy sauce
2 teaspoons sesame oil
freshly ground black pepper, to taste
2 teaspoons cornflour

P Can be prepared ahead: cover and refrigerate the pork for up to 2 hours.

1 Cut the pork into thin slices 5 x 1cm (2 x ½ in). In a medium-sized bowl, combine the marinade ingredients. Add the pork, mix well and marinate for 15 minutes at room temperature. Drain, discarding the marinade. P

2 Heat a wok on high heat until it is hot. Add the oil, and when it is very hot and slightly smoking, add the pork slices and brown undisturbed for 30 seconds. Then stir-fry until cooked (about 2 minutes). Make sure that there is no pink left. Remove with a slotted spoon and leave to drain in a colander.

3 Reheat the wok over a high heat and when it is hot, add the cashew nuts, salt, pepper and sugar. Reduce the heat to low and stir-fry for 2 minutes.

4 Return the pork to the wok and stir-fry for 2 minutes or until heated through.

5 Turn onto a warm platter and serve at once.

This is a delectable way to prepare beef with an unusual flavour. The beef is hardened in the freezer and then tenderised in a marinade. The final cooking is a matter of minutes.

orange-flavoured beef

450g (1 lb) lean beef fillet or steak

4 tablespoons groundnut (peanut) oil

350g (12 oz) finely sliced onion

3 tablespoons coarsely chopped garlic

2 tablespoons orange zest

2 tablespoons Shaoxing rice wine or dry
    sherry

salt and freshly ground black pepper, to taste

2 teaspoons sugar

2 tablespoons oyster sauce

MARINADE

2 teaspoons light soy sauce

2 teaspoons Shaoxing rice wine or dry
    sherry

2 teaspoons sesame oil

salt and freshly ground black pepper, to taste

2 teaspoons cornflour

P Can be prepared ahead: cover and
refrigerate the beef for up to 2 hours.

1 Put the beef in the freezing compartment of the refrigerator for 20 minutes. This will allow the meat to harden slightly for easier cutting.

2 While the beef is hardening, make the marinade by combining the ingredients in a medium-sized bowl.

3 When the beef has been in the freezer for 20 minutes, remove and cut into thin slices 4cm (1½ in) long. Add to the marinade, mix well and marinate for 15 minutes at room temperature. Drain, discarding the marinade. P

4 Heat a wok over high heat until it is very hot. Add 3 tablespoons of the oil, and when it is very hot and slightly smoking, add the beef and stir-fry for about 2 minutes. Remove the beef and drain in a colander.

5 Reheat the wok over high heat. When it is very hot, add the remaining oil, then the onion, garlic and orange zest, and stir-fry for 1 minute.

6 Now add the rice wine or sherry, salt, pepper and sugar. Continue to stir-fry for 3 minutes or until the onion is tender. If it becomes too dry, add a tablespoon or so of water as necessary. Quickly return the beef to the wok, add the oyster sauce and stir well until heated through.

7 Turn onto a warm platter and serve at once.

This is the recipe I turn to when I want a very quick meal that is elegant at the same time. The marinating, which accounts for all the preparation time, can be done in advance, and the cooking time includes 10 minutes of 'resting time'. However, you must buy the best and most tender beef fillets.

pan-fried beef with oyster sauce

4 tender beef fillets, about 175–225g
   (6–8 oz) each
salt and freshly ground black pepper, to taste
3 tablespoons groundnut (peanut) oil
2 tablespoons oyster sauce, per fillet

MARINADE
3 tablespoons light soy sauce
2 tablespoons sesame oil

P Can be prepared ahead: cover and refrigerate the beef for up to 2 hours.

1 Lay the fillets in a shallow dish. In a medium-sized bowl, combine the marinade ingredients and coat the fillets evenly with this on both sides. Then season both sides well with salt and pepper. Marinate at room temperature for at least 1 hour. Drain, discarding the marinade. **P**

2 Heat a wok over high heat until it is hot. Add the oil, turn the heat down to moderate and pan-fry the fillets for 4–8 minutes on each side, depending how well you like your beef done. Transfer to a warm platter and allow to rest for 10 minutes. This 'relaxes' the beef and makes it tender.

3 Immediately before serving, slice the fillets and pour 2 tablespoons of oyster sauce over each one.

This is a quick and easy version of a great Chinese favourite that my mother use to make. It is comfort food at its best. Most of the preparation time is for draining the beancurd, to ensure that it is not too wet. An added bonus is that this dish can be cooked ahead of time and then gently reheated.

braised beef with beancurd

450g (1 lb) fresh firm beancurd

1½ tablespoons groundnut (peanut) oil

2 tablespoons coarsely chopped garlic

1 tablespoon finely chopped fresh ginger

350g (12 oz) minced beef

3 tablespoons finely chopped spring onions

2 tablespoons oyster sauce

2 teaspoons chilli bean sauce

1 teaspoon sugar

1½ tablespoons Shaoxing rice wine or dry sherry

1 tablespoon light soy sauce

50ml (2 fl oz) home-made chicken stock (see page 23) or quality store-bought fresh stock

GARNISH

2 tablespoons finely chopped spring onions

P Can be prepared ahead: cover and refrigerate for up to 12 hours. Reheat gently in a steamer for 10 minutes.

1 Cut the beancurd into 1cm (½ in) cubes and put into a sieve to drain for 10 minutes. Then lay on kitchen paper to drain for another 10 minutes.

2 Heat a wok over high heat until it is hot. Add the oil, and when it is very hot and slightly smoking, add the garlic and ginger, and stir-fry for 20 seconds.

3 Add the minced beef and stir-fry for 3 minutes.

4 Now add all the other ingredients except the beancurd, and bring to the boil.

5 Turn the heat down to low, add the beancurd and mix it in well, but gently, taking care not to break up the chunks. Simmer slowly, uncovered, for about 15 minutes. If necessary, add a little more stock. P

6 Turn onto a warm platter, garnish with the spring onions and serve at once.

vegetables

SERVES 4 AS A SIDE DISH

PREPARATION TIME: 10 MINUTES

COOKING TIME: 4–5 MINUTES

Crispy and tender, with a wonderful earthy flavour, asparagus is a recent discovery for many Chinese cooks. It resembles what we know as rice shoots. Here the asparagus is blanched, cooled and tossed in an easy-to-make sauce. It is always best not to add the sauce until the moment you are ready to serve the salad.

Chinese-style asparagus salad

450g (1 lb) asparagus
3 tablespoons finely chopped shallots
1 tablespoon sesame seeds

DRESSING
2 tablespoons light soy sauce
salt and freshly ground black pepper, to taste
1 tablespoon sesame oil
1–2 teaspoons chilli oil

P Can be prepared ahead: put the dressing in a screw-topped jar and refrigerate; it will keep for 2 days. Cover the asparagus and refrigerate for up to 2 hours. Put the seeds in a screw-topped jar, where they will keep for 2 days.

1 First, make the soy dressing. In a small bowl, combine all the ingredients for the dressing. Mix well and set aside.

2 Cut the asparagus into 4cm (1½ in) pieces. Put the chopped shallots in a clean teatowel and squeeze out until dry. Set aside.

3 Place the sesame seeds on a baking tray and put under a hot grill until golden brown. Watch them to make sure they do not burn. Set aside. P

4 Bring a wok of salted water to the boil. Now add the asparagus, bring the water back to the boil and cook for 4 minutes or until tender. Remove the asparagus with a slotted spoon and plunge it immediately into cold water. Leave for a few minutes to cool, then drain well. When cold, turn the asparagus onto a platter.

5 When you are ready to serve, drizzle with the soy dressing. Add the shallots and toss well. Sprinkle with the sesame seeds and serve at once.

This is another delicious method of enjoying aubergines. Here they are cooked in a gentle steam and then tossed in a savoury sauce that is easy to make. This vegetarian delight makes a terrific accompaniment to any meal, with the added bonus that the first part of the recipe can be completed in advance.

cold aubergine salad

450g (1 lb) aubergines

SAUCE

1½ tablespoons sesame oil

1–2 teaspoons chilli oil

2 tablespoons finely chopped garlic

1½ tablespoons finely chopped fresh ginger

3 tablespoons finely chopped spring onions

2 tablespoons light soy sauce

1 tablespoon sugar

1 tablespoon Chinese black rice vinegar

GARNISH

handful fresh coriander sprigs (optional)

P Can be prepared ahead: cover and refrigerate the aubergines for up to 24 hours. Bring back to room temperature before completing the recipe.

1 Cut the aubergines into large 5cm (2 in) squares. Do not peel them.

2 Next, set up a steamer or put a rack into a wok and fill it with 5cm (2 in) of water. Bring the water to the boil over a high heat. Put the aubergines onto a heatproof plate and carefully lower it into the steamer or onto the rack. Turn the heat down to low and cover the wok tightly. Steam gently for 30–40 minutes or until the aubergines are very soft to the touch. When they are cooked, remove from the wok, transfer to a platter and allow to cool thoroughly. P

3 Now make the sauce. Wipe the wok clean and reheat it. When it is hot, add the sesame and chilli oils. When they are very hot and slightly smoking, add the garlic and stir-fry for 40 seconds.

4 Add the rest of the ingredients, mix thoroughly and stir-fry for 1 minute. Remove the wok from the heat and allow the sauce to cool.

5 When you are ready to serve, pour the sauce evenly over the aubergines and toss well. Garnish with the coriander if using and serve at once at room temperature.

This delicious aubergine purée was inspired by a good friend, Mic Cheminal-Teran, a well-known French designer of costumes for theatre and cinema. To make this dish for vegetarians, use vegetarian oyster sauce (see page 18). Serve cold or at room temperature. This is one recipe where you won't need your wok!

Mic's aubergine purée

900g (2 lb) aubergines
3 tablespoons finely chopped spring
onions
2 tablespoons finely chopped garlic
2 tablespoons oyster sauce
2 tablespoons extra-virgin olive oil
1 teaspoon sugar
salt and freshly ground black pepper, to taste

P Can be prepared ahead: cover and refrigerate for up to 24 hours. Bring back to room temperature before serving.

1 Preheat the oven to 240°C, 475°F, gas mark 9.

2 Using a fork, prick the skins of the aubergines; this will prevent them exploding while they are cooking. Leave them whole. Lay them on a greased baking tray and roast for about 30–40 minutes or until they are soft and cooked through. Allow to cool.

3 When they are cool enough to handle, peel off and discard the skins. Put the flesh into a colander and allow to drain for 30 minutes or more.

4 When completely cold, mash into a purée with a fork. This can be done several hours in advance. If preparing ahead, cover and refrigerate. P

5 In a large bowl, combine the rest of the ingredients.

6 Add the aubergine purée, mix well and serve at once.

SERVES 4

PREPARATION TIME: 25 MINUTES

COOKING TIME: 5–6 MINUTES

This unusual and delightful recipe comes from the imaginative and creative Andy Wai of the Harbor Village Restaurant in San Francisco. You can find bitter melon in Chinese and Asian supermarkets, or use courgettes, which are prepared in exactly the same way.

Andy Wai's bitter melon omelette

450g (1 lb) bitter melon or courgettes

1 tablespoon plus 1 teaspoon salt

6 eggs, beaten

1 teaspoon light soy sauce

2 teaspoons sesame oil

1½ tablespoons groundnut (peanut) oil

1 Wash the bitter melon or courgettes and cut in half lengthwise. Remove the seeds and cut the flesh into fine slices. In a bowl, mix with 1 tablespoon of the salt. Turn into a colander and stand for 20 minutes. Rinse well in cold water and drain.

2 Bring a large saucepan of water to the boil. Slip in the melon slices, bring back to the boil and blanch for 1 minute. Remove with a slotted spoon and drain well on kitchen paper.

3 Combine the eggs with the remaining salt, soy sauce and sesame oil. Add the melon slices.

4 Heat a wok over high heat until it is hot. Add the oil, and when it is very hot and slightly smoking, add the egg mixture. Gather the edges into the middle, letting the liquid egg run underneath, and continue to cook until it sets. Then flip the omelette over and cook the other side until it is golden brown.

5 Serve at once while hot.

Chinese fermented black beans are delicious with almost any food. They can easily transform an everyday vegetable into a savoury treat. Again, this is a recipe where all the work can be done in advance.

baby corn with black beans and chilli

225g (8 oz) red peppers (about 1)

1½ tablespoons groundnut (peanut) oil

3 tablespoons finely chopped shallots

2 tablespoons black beans, coarsely chopped

1½ tablespoons finely chopped garlic

1 tablespoon finely chopped fresh ginger

225g (8 oz) fresh baby corn

2 tablespoons Shaoxing rice wine or dry sherry

1 tablespoon chilli bean sauce

1 tablespoon light soy sauce

2 tablespoons dark soy sauce

2 teaspoons sugar

150ml (5 fl oz) home-made chicken stock (see page 23) or quality store-bought fresh stock

2 teaspoons sesame oil

1 Cut the red peppers in half and remove the white pith and seeds. Cut into 2.5cm (1 in) pieces.

2 Heat a wok over high heat until it is hot, then add the oil. When it is hot and slightly smoking, add the shallots, black beans, garlic and ginger, and stir-fry for 1 minute.

3 Add the baby corn and stir-fry for 1 minute.

4 Add the rice wine or sherry, chilli bean sauce, soy sauces, sugar and stock, and continue to stir-fry over high heat for 5 minutes, or until the corn is tender and most of the liquid has evaporated.

5 Finally stir in the sesame oil and mix in well. Turn onto a platter and allow to cool. **P**

6 Serve at room temperature.

P Can be prepared ahead: cover the corn and refrigerate for up to 23 hours. Bring back to room temperature before serving.

SERVES 4 AS A SIDE DISH

PREPARATION TIME: 5 MINUTES

COOKING TIME: 12 MINUTES

This is yet another delicious way to cook green beans, but this time as a treat for meat eaters.

savoury stir-fried beans with bacon

175g (6 oz) streaky bacon

450g (1 lb) French or dwarf beans or haricots verts, trimmed

2 tablespoons groundnut (peanut) oil

1 teaspoon sugar

1 tablespoon light soy sauce

3 tablespoons water

salt and freshly ground black pepper, to taste

2 teaspoons sesame oil

1 Cut the bacon into thin shreds. If the beans are more than 7.5cm (3 in) long, slice them. Otherwise, keep them whole.

2 Heat a wok over high heat until it is hot. Turn the heat down to low, add the bacon and stir-fry until it is brown and crispy. Remove with a slotted spoon and drain well on kitchen paper.

3 Wipe out the wok with kitchen paper and reheat it over high heat until it is hot. Add the oil, and when it is very hot and slightly smoking, add the beans and stir-fry for 30 seconds.

4 Add the sugar, soy sauce and water, and continue to stir-fry for 1 minute.

5 Add the salt and pepper, cover the wok tightly and simmer for 5 minutes or until the beans are tender. Check from time to time, adding more water if necessary.

6 When the beans are fully cooked, uncover the wok and continue to stir-fry until all the liquid has evaporated.

7 Finally, stir in the sesame oil. Immediately remove the wok from the heat.

8 Arrange the beans on a warm platter, garnish with the bacon and serve at once.

SERVES 2 AS A MAIN COURSE,
4 AS A SIDE DISH

PREPARATION TIME: 3 MINUTES

COOKING TIME: 10 MINUTES

A true vegetarian treat that is as tasty as any meat dish. Here fresh green beans, quickly stir-fried in a hot wok, are paired with fermented beancurd. This inexpensive condiment, available from Chinese grocers, is well worth searching for, especially if you are looking for a different vegetarian taste.

stir-fried beans with chilli beancurd

450g (1 lb) French or dwarf beans or
  haricots verts, trimmed
1½ tablespoons groundnut (peanut) oil
3 tablespoons fermented beancurd with
  chilli
6 tablespoons water
1 teaspoon sugar

1 If the beans are more than 7.5cm (3 in) long, slice them. Otherwise, keep them whole.

2 Heat a wok over high heat until it is hot. Add the oil, and when it is very hot and slightly smoking, add the beans and fermented beancurd, and stir-fry for 30 seconds.

3 Add 3 tablespoons of the water and continue to stir-fry for 1 minute.

4 Add the sugar, cover the wok tightly and simmer for 5 minutes or until the beans are fully cooked. Check from time to time, adding the additional 3 tablespoons of water if necessary.

5 When the beans are tender, uncover the wok and stir-fry until all the liquid has evaporated.

6 Turn onto a warm platter and serve at once.

SERVES 4–6 AS A SIDE DISH

PREPARATION TIME: 3 MINUTES

COOKING TIME: 5–7 MINUTES

This is a delectable, healthy and easy courgette dish that is cooked in minutes in the wok. You can serve it either as a satisfying vegetarian dish on its own or as a tasty accompaniment to any meal.

curried courgettes

675g (1½ lb) courgettes, ends trimmed

2 tablespoons groundnut (peanut) oil

3 tablespoons coarsely chopped garlic

50g (2 oz) sliced onions

2 tablespoons Madras curry powder

1 tablespoon Shaoxing rice wine or dry sherry

6 tablespoons water

2 teaspoons sesame oil

1 Cut the courgettes into 2.5cm (1 in) cubes.

2 Heat a wok over high heat until it is hot, then add the oil. When it is hot, add the garlic and onions, and stir-fry for 30 seconds.

3 Add the courgettes and stir-fry for 2 minutes.

4 Add the curry powder, rice wine or sherry and 3 tablespoons of the water. Cover the pan or wok and continue to cook for 3–5 minutes or until the courgettes are tender. Check from time to time, adding the additional 3 tablespoons of water if necessary.

5 Finally, stir in the sesame oil.

6 Turn onto a warm platter and serve at once.

SERVES 2 AS A MAIN COURSE,
4 AS A SIDE DISH
PREPARATION TIME: 10 MINUTES
COOKING TIME: 35 MINUTES

In Chinese cuisine, many braised meat dishes are slowly simmered in a broth seasoned with aromatic spices such as star anise and cinnamon, to produce a dish redolent with fragrant, mouth-watering flavours. In this vegetarian version, the same technique is used with root vegetables.

fragrant braised vegetables

450g (1 lb) carrots
225g (8 oz) turnips
225g (8 oz) potatoes
2 star anise
1 cinnamon stick
1 tablespoon light soy sauce
1½ tablespoons dark soy sauce
1 tablespoon Shaoxing rice wine or dry
   sherry
2 tablespoons rock sugar or granulated
   sugar
600ml (1 pint) home-made vegetarian
   stock (see page 24) or quality store-
   bought fresh stock

GARNISH
2 tablespoons finely chopped fresh
   coriander

P Can be prepared ahead: cover and refrigerate for up to 24 hours. To reheat, heat gently in a wok for 10 minutes, or until heated through.

1 Peel the carrots and roll-cut them (see page 21) into 2.5cm (1 in) lengths. Peel the turnips and potatoes and cut into 2.5cm (1 in) cubes.

2 In a wok, combine the star anise, cinnamon, soy sauces, rice wine or sherry, sugar and stock, and bring to simmering point. Add the carrots and potatoes, and simmer for 15 minutes or until they are tender.

3 Then add the turnips and continue to simmer for another 15 minutes or until all the vegetables are tender.

4 Remove the vegetables with a slotted spoon. Reduce the sauce over high heat until it has turned into a syrup.

5 Return the vegetables to the wok and stir well to heat through and coat thoroughly with the sauce. P

6 Turn onto a warm platter, garnish with the coriander and serve at once.

SERVES 4 AS A SIDE DISH

PREPARATION TIME: 10 MINUTES

COOKING TIME: 7 MINUTES

Nothing could be quicker, simpler or tastier than this exciting combination of spinach and ginger. The secret is to stir-fry the ginger until it is brown and slightly crispy. The result is a vegetarian delight that is also a delectable accompaniment to any meat dish.

stir-fried spinach with ginger

750g (1½ lb) fresh spinach
1 tablespoon extra-virgin olive oil
1 tablespoon groundnut (peanut) oil
3 tablespoons finely chopped fresh ginger
salt, to taste
1 teaspoon sugar
freshly ground black pepper, to taste

1 Wash the spinach thoroughly in at least two changes of cold water. Remove all the stems and discard, retaining just the leaves.

2 Heat a wok over high heat until it is hot. Add the oils, and when they are very hot and slightly smoking, add the ginger and salt, and stir-fry for 10 seconds or until brown and crispy.

3 Then add the spinach and stir-fry for about 2 minutes so that it is thoroughly coated with the oil, ginger and salt.

4 When the spinach has wilted to about one-third of its original size, add the sugar and pepper, and continue to stir-fry for another 4 minutes.

5 Transfer the spinach to a colander to drain off any excess liquid.

6 Turn onto a warm platter and serve at once.

This version of tempura originated in the kitchens of The Oriental in Bangkok. The classic Japanese tempura originally derived from a word meaning 'to season' but now it has come to mean coating fresh foods in a light, delicate batter. Most of the preparation time is taken up with draining the beancurd.

vegetable and beancurd tempura

100g (4 oz) fresh firm beancurd
100g (4 oz) cauliflower
100g (4 oz) courgettes
100g (4 oz) carrots
100g (4 oz) aubergines
50g (2 oz) Chinese long beans, runner
  beans or haricots verts, trimmed
100g (4 oz) onions
100g (4 oz) small button mushrooms
plain flour, for dusting
600ml (1 pint) groundnut (peanut) oil
salt and freshly ground black pepper, to taste

BATTER
2 egg yolks
300ml (10 fl oz) iced water
200g (7 oz) plain flour, sifted

1 Drain the beancurd and cut it into small 2.5cm (1 in) cubes. Set on kitchen paper to drain further for 30 minutes.

2 While it is draining, prepare the vegetables. Cut the cauliflower into small florets about 4cm (1½ in) wide. Cut the courgettes, carrots and aubergines into thin slices 10cm (4 in) long. Cut the beans into 10cm (4 in) lengths. Thinly slice the onion. Wipe the mushrooms but leave whole. Dust all the vegetables lightly with flour, shaking off all the excess.

3 Heat the oil in a large wok until it is hot. While it is heating, make the batter. In a medium-sized bowl, lightly beat the egg yolks, then add the iced water and mix lightly twice. Then add all the flour at once, beating a few times until the batter is just combined but still lumpy.

4 Dip the vegetables in the batter and deep-fry in several batches until golden and crispy. Remove with a slotted spoon, drain on kitchen paper. Repeat with the remaining batches.

5 When all the vegetables are cooked, turn onto a warm platter. Sprinkle with salt and pepper, and serve at once.

vegetables 123

SERVES 4 AS A SIDE DISH

PREPARATION TIME: 2 HOURS,
    INCLUDING COOLING TIME

COOKING TIME: 25 MINUTES

The fact that Chinese five-spice powder is now available in supermarkets means that everyone can try this exotic but delectable version of chips that is quick and easy too. If you can, use Maldon sea salt; it adds immeasurably to the flavour.

five-spice chips

750g (1½ lb) potatoes
900ml (1½ pints) groundnut (peanut) oil

SPICE MIX
2 teaspoons Maldon sea salt or ordinary
    salt
1 teaspoon five-spice powder
½ teaspoon Madras curry powder
freshly ground black pepper, to taste

P Can be prepared ahead, in two stages if wished: complete to the end of stage 1; cover the potatoes and refrigerate for 24 hours. Then prepare to the end of stage 4 up to 1 hour before completing the recipe.

1 Peel the potatoes and cut into strips about 7.5 x 1cm (3 x ½ in). Put into a large bowl and cover with cold water. Refrigerate for 2 hours or overnight. **P**

2 Combine the spice mixture ingredients in a small bowl and set aside.

3 Drain the potatoes in a colander, then spin them dry in a salad spinner or pat dry with kitchen paper. They should be as dry as possible. Divide into two batches.

4 Heat a wok over high heat until it is hot. Add the oil, and when it is very hot and slightly smoking, deep-fry the first batch for 8 minutes. Remove with a slotted spoon and drain in a colander. Repeat for the second batch. **P**

5 When you are ready to serve them, reheat the oil again until it is very hot. Fry the first batch until they are crispy and golden brown. Remove and drain well on kitchen paper. Reheat the oil until it is very hot and repeat for the second batch.

6 Transfer to a warm platter and toss with half of the spice mix. Taste and add more if you desire. Serve at once.

A delicious vegetarian treat. Don't be put off by the long list of ingredients. Most of the work can be done in advance (up to the end of stage 3), leaving only the final part to be done just before serving. This dish is great fun to eat and also makes a good finger-food starter for a dinner party.

stir-fried vegetables in lettuce cups

15g (½ oz) Chinese dried mushrooms
100g (4 oz) carrots
100g (4 oz) fresh or tinned bamboo shoots
100g (4 oz) courgettes
100g (4 oz) celery hearts
100g (4 oz) red or green pepper (about 1)
100g (4 oz) pressed seasoned beancurd
225g (8 oz) iceberg lettuce
1½ tablespoons groundnut (peanut) oil
1 tablespoon coarsely chopped garlic
3 tablespoons finely chopped shallots
3 tablespoons finely chopped spring onions
2 teaspoons light soy sauce
2 teaspoons Shaoxing rice wine or dry sherry
3 tablespoons vegetarian oyster sauce
salt and freshly ground black pepper, to taste

TO SERVE
4 tablespoons hoisin sauce

> **P** Can be prepared ahead: prepare the vegetables up to the end of stage 3, cover and refrigerate for up to 6 hours.

1 Soak the dried mushrooms in warm water for 20 minutes.

2 While the mushrooms are soaking, prepare the vegetables. Peel the carrots and cut into fine shreds 5cm (2 in) long. Shred the bamboo shoots, courgettes and celery hearts in the same way. Cut the peppers in half, remove the white pith and seeds, and shred too. Finely shred the pressed beancurd. Separate the lettuce into leaves and wash. Dry in a salad spinner and set aside, covered, in the refrigerator.

3 When the mushrooms have soaked for 20 minutes, drain them and discard the water. Squeeze out any excess liquid. Trim off the stems and discard. Shred the caps into strips 5cm (2 in) long. **P**

4 Heat a wok over high heat until it is hot. Add the oil, and when it is very hot and slightly smoking, add the garlic, shallots and spring onions and stir-fry for 20 seconds.

5 Add the carrots and stir-fry for 1 further minute.

6 Now add the remaining vegetables (except the lettuce), the soy sauce, rice wine or sherry, vegetarian oyster sauce, salt and pepper, and stir-fry the mixture for 3 minutes.

7 Turn onto a warm platter. Arrange the lettuce on a separate platter, put the hoisin sauce into a small bowl, and serve at once. Each guest places a portion of stir-fried vegetables in a lettuce leaf, adds a little hoisin sauce, wraps the leaf around and eats with their fingers.

I created this recipe for my demonstration vegetarian menu at The Oriental in Bangkok. Served with a light vegetarian broth instead of a heavy sauce it makes for a healthy but satisfying vegetarian dish. It is best cooked in a non-stick wok.

savoury stuffed beancurd

450g (1 lb) fresh firm beancurd
2½ tablespoons extra-virgin olive oil

STUFFING
2 tablespoons coarsely chopped garlic
3 tablespoons finely diced carrots
25g (1 oz) finely diced button mushrooms
3 tablespoons finely diced courgettes
2 tablespoons seeded and finely chopped
  fresh red chillies
2 tablespoons finely chopped spring onions
2 tablespoons finely chopped chives
2 tablespoons finely chopped fresh
  coriander
3 tablespoons finely chopped roasted
  cashew nuts
2 tablespoons finely chopped fresh basil
salt and freshly ground black pepper, to taste

SAUCE
100ml (3½ fl oz) home-made vegetarian
  stock (see page 24) or quality store-
  bought fresh stock
3 tablespoons vegetarian oyster sauce

1 Drain the beancurd and cut it into squares 5 x 2.5cm (2 x 1 in) thick. Set on kitchen paper to drain further for 30 minutes.

2 Next, make the stuffing. Heat a wok on high heat until it is hot. Add 1 tablespoon of the olive oil, turn the heat down and add the garlic. Stir-fry for 30 seconds or until slightly brown. Add the carrots, mushrooms, courgettes and chillies, and stir-fry for 3 minutes.

3 Add the spring onions, chives, coriander, cashew nuts, basil, salt and pepper, mix well and remove from the heat. Turn into a bowl and allow to cool thoroughly.

4 Turn the beancurd squares on their sides. With a teaspoon, scoop out a small pocket in the centre of the longest side. Be careful not to break them up. Place a spoonful of the cooked stuffing in each pocket.

5 Heat a non-stick wok until it is hot. Add the remaining olive oil and turn the temperature down to its lowest heat. Gently pan-fry the squares, undisturbed, for about 8–10 minutes or until they are golden brown.

6 Cover the pan tightly and continue to cook, undisturbed, for 5 minutes. Remove the squares and drain well on kitchen paper for about 1 minute. Carefully turn onto a warm serving platter.

7 Reheat the wok over a high heat and when it is hot, add the stock and vegetarian oyster sauce, and heat through. Pour the sauce over the beancurd and serve at once.

SERVES 2–4 AS A SIDE DISH
PREPARATION TIME: 5 MINUTES
COOKING TIME: 8–10 MINUTES

Green beans are never better than when quickly stir-fried in the wok and perfumed by fragrant garlic. A perfect vegetarian dish that is a great accompaniment as well.

stir-fried green beans with garlic

450g (1 lb) French or dwarf beans or
   haricots verts, trimmed
1½ tablespoons groundnut (peanut) oil
3 tablespoons finely sliced garlic
salt and freshly ground black pepper, to taste
1 teaspoon sugar
3 tablespoons Shaoxing rice wine or dry
   sherry

1 If the beans are more than 7.5cm (3 in) long, slice them. Otherwise, keep them whole.

2 Heat a wok over high heat until it is hot. Add the oil, and when it is very hot and slightly smoking, add the garlic and stir-fry for 30 seconds.

3 Add the beans, salt, pepper, sugar and rice wine or sherry, and continue to stir-fry for 1 minute.

4 Cover the wok and simmer for 5 minutes or until the beans are fully cooked, adding another tablespoon of rice wine or sherry or water from time to time as needed.

5 Uncover the wok and continue to stir-fry until all the liquid is evaporated.

6 Turn onto a warm platter and serve at once.

noodles and rice

The rice in this recipe needs to be pre-cooked because otherwise it will not stir-fry properly. Hot rice, when it hits a hot wok, tends to absorb all the oil and 'melts' into sticky lumps. Once it has cooled, however, the starch can 'settle', which prevents sticking. This dish is equally good served cold.

pineapple rice

long-grain white rice, measured to the 400ml (14 fl oz) level in a measuring jug and cooked according to the method given on page 26 for Steamed Rice
2 tablespoons groundnut (peanut) oil
2 tablespoons coarsely chopped garlic
2 teaspoons finely chopped ginger
175g (6 oz) minced beef or pork
salt and freshly ground black pepper, to taste
225g (8 oz) fresh or tinned pineapple, chopped
3 tablespoons finely chopped spring onions

P Can be prepared ahead: cover the rice and refrigerate for up to 24 hours.

1 First cook your rice at least 2 hours ahead or the night before. Allow it to cool thoroughly by spreading it on a baking sheet. When it is cool, cover and refrigerate. When the rice is completely cold, proceed with the rest of the recipe. **P**

2 Heat a wok over a high heat until it is hot. Add the oil, and when it is very hot and slightly smoking, add the garlic and ginger and stir-fry for 20 seconds.

3 Add the beef or pork and stir-fry for 2 minutes. Then add the cooked rice and stir-fry for 3 minutes or until it is thoroughly heated through. Season well with salt and pepper.

4 Now add the pineapple and continue to stir-fry for 2–3 minutes. Finally, toss in the spring onions and stir several times.

5 Turn onto a warm platter and serve at once.

SERVES 4 AS A MAIN COURSE,
OR 6 AS A SIDE DISH
PREPARATION TIME: 2 HOURS,
INCLUDING COOLING TIME
COOKING TIME: 10 MINUTES

This is my vegetarian version of the famous nasi goreng – a tasty Indonesian rice dish. I have retained the traditional fried eggs, but you can easily omit them if you want a lighter meal. As with the recipe on page 132, the rice should be cooked several hours in advance, or even the night before.

vegetarian nasi goreng

long-grain white rice, measured to the
    400ml (14 fl oz) level in a measuring jug
    and cooked according to the method
    given on page 26 for Steamed Rice
2 eggs
2 teaspoons sesame oil
salt, to taste
2 tablespoons groundnut (peanut) oil
2 tablespoons coarsely chopped garlic
1 finely chopped onion
2 teaspoons finely chopped fresh ginger
freshly ground black pepper, to taste
1 teaspoon sugar
2 tablespoons vegetarian oyster sauce
1 tablespoon chilli bean sauce
1 tablespoon dark soy sauce

GARNISH
1 tablespoon groundnut (peanut) oil
2 eggs
3 tablespoons finely chopped spring onions
handful fresh coriander sprigs

P Can be prepared ahead: cover the rice
and refrigerate for up to 24 hours.

1 First cook your rice at least 2 hours ahead or the night before. Allow it to cool thoroughly by spreading it on a baking sheet. When it is cool, cover and refrigerate. When the rice is completely cold, proceed with the rest of the recipe. **P**

2 In a small bowl, beat the eggs with the sesame oil and a little salt. Set aside.

3 Heat a wok over high heat until it is hot. Add the groundnut oil, and when it is very hot and slightly smoking, add the garlic, onion, ginger, salt and pepper, and stir-fry for 2 minutes.

4 Add the rice and stir-fry for 3 minutes.

5 Add the sugar, vegetarian oyster sauce, chilli bean sauce and soy sauce, and stir-fry for 2 minutes.

6 Add the egg mixture and continue to stir-fry for 1 further minute. Turn onto a warm platter and set aside.

7 Finally, make the garnish. Wipe the wok clean with kitchen paper and reheat it. When it is hot, add the oil. When it is hot and slightly smoking, fry the eggs.

8 Using a slotted spoon, place the cooked eggs on top of the rice and sprinkle with the spring onions and coriander. Serve at once.

Nothing could be simpler or tastier than this recipe combining rice and prawns. The great bonus is that the finished dish reheats well. As in the two previous recipes, the rice needs to be cooked several hours in advance or even the night before, for the same practical reasons.

prawn rice

long-grain white rice, measured to the
    400ml (14 fl oz) level in a measuring jug
    and cooked according to the method
    given on page 26 for Steamed Rice
225g (8 oz) raw unpeeled prawns, fresh
    or frozen
2 tablespoons groundnut (peanut) oil
2 tablespoons coarsely chopped garlic
2 teaspoons finely chopped fresh ginger
salt and freshly ground black pepper, to taste
2 large eggs
2 teaspoons sesame oil
3 tablespoons finely chopped spring onions

1 First cook your rice at least 2 hours ahead or the night before. Allow it to cool thoroughly by spreading it on a baking sheet. When it is cool, cover and refrigerate. When the rice is completely cold, proceed with the rest of the recipe.

2 If using frozen prawns, defrost thoroughly. Peel the prawns and discard the shells. Using a small sharp knife, remove the fine digestive cord. Wash them, drain and pat dry with kitchen paper. Chop coarsely.

3 Heat a wok over high heat until it is hot. Add the oil, and when it is very hot and slightly smoking, add the garlic, ginger, salt and pepper, and stir-fry for 20 seconds.

4 Add the prawns and cooked rice, and stir-fry for 3 minutes or until thoroughly heated through.

5 In a small bowl, quickly combine the eggs and sesame oil with some salt. Drizzle this into the rice and continue to stir-fry for 2–3 minutes or until the eggs have set and the liquid has evaporated.

6 Toss in the spring onions and stir several times.

7 Turn onto a warm platter and serve at once.

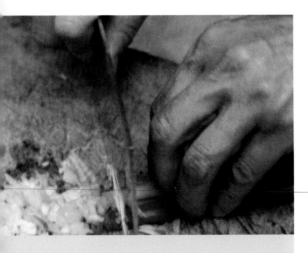

This is a quick and delicious combination of everyone's favourite – noodles – with delectable broccoli. The noodles can be prepared ahead up to the end of stage 1 and will keep in the fridge for up to 24 hours.

tasty noodles with broccoli

225g (8 oz) dried or fresh egg noodles
1 tablespoon plus 2 teaspoons sesame oil
450g (1 lb) fresh broccoli
1½ tablespoons groundnut (peanut) oil
3 tablespoons coarsely chopped garlic
salt and freshly ground black pepper, to taste
2 tablespoons Shaoxing rice wine or dry sherry
1 tablespoon chilli bean sauce
1 teaspoon sugar
4–5 tablespoons water

1 Cook the noodles for 3–5 minutes in a large pot of boiling water. Then immerse in cold water just for a few seconds, to stop them from cooking further, and drain thoroughly. Toss with 1 tablespoon sesame oil and set aside.

2 Separate the broccoli heads into small florets. Peel and slice the stems wafer-thin (2.5mm or ⅛ in). Blanch the broccoli pieces in a large pot of boiling salted water for 3 minutes. Immerse them in cold water for 2 minutes or until just cool, and drain thoroughly.

3 Heat a wok over high heat until it is hot. Add the oil, and when it is very hot and slightly smoking, add the garlic and stir-fry for 20 seconds. Add the salt, pepper, rice wine or sherry, chilli bean sauce and sugar, and stir-fry for another 20 seconds.

4 Add the broccoli together with 2–3 tablespoons of the water. Stir-fry at a moderate to high heat for 4 minutes or until the broccoli is thoroughly heated through. Add more water if necessary.

5 Add the cooked noodles and stir well.

6 Finally, add the remaining sesame oil and continue to stir-fry for 30 seconds.

7 Turn onto a warm platter and serve at once.

A very popular noodle dish to be found all over Thailand, this is a symphony of sweet, sour, spicy and savoury tastes all at the same time. There are as many variations on this dish as there are cooks. This vegetarian version without the traditional dried shrimps is just as delectable as the original.

stir-fried vegetarian phad Thai

225g (8 oz) flat dried rice noodles
50g (2 oz) shallots
100g (4 oz) onions
4 spring onions
3 fresh red chillies (or green ones if you want a 'hotter' dish)
2 tablespoons groundnut (peanut) oil
3 tablespoons coarsely chopped garlic
3 tablespoons fish sauce or light soy sauce
1 tablespoon Shaoxing rice wine or dry sherry
1 tablespoon lime juice
1 tablespoon light soy sauce
salt and freshly ground black pepper, to taste
1 tablespoon sugar
2 tablespoons vegetarian oyster sauce
225g (8 oz) fresh beansprouts
handful fresh coriander sprigs

GARNISH
3 tablespoons coarsely chopped roasted peanuts

1 Soak the rice noodles in a bowl of hot water for 25 minutes.

2 While the noodles are soaking, prepare the vegetables. Peel and thinly slice the shallots and onion. Slice the spring onions at a slight angle into 2.5cm (1 in) lengths. Seed and finely chop the chillies.

3 When the noodles have soaked for 25 minutes, drain well in a colander or sieve. Discard the water.

4 Heat a wok over high heat. When it is hot, add the oil. When it is very hot and slightly smoking, add the shallots, onion, spring onions, chillies and garlic, and stir-fry for 1 minute.

5 Add the rice noodles, fish sauce or soy sauce, rice wine or sherry, lime juice, soy sauce, pepper, sugar and vegetarian oyster sauce, and continue to stir-fry for 2 minutes, mixing well.

6 Add the beansprouts and continue to stir-fry for 4 minutes.

7 Finally, add the coriander and stir-fry briskly for 30 seconds.

8 Turn onto a warm platter, sprinkle with the peanuts and serve at once.

SERVES 2–4 AS A SIDE DISH

PREPARATION TIME: 2 HOURS,
    INCLUDING COOLING TIME

COOKING TIME: 12 MINUTES

This is my vegetarian interpretation of a delicious rice dish created by one of my Malaysian cooks. As with the earlier rice dishes, the rice needs to be cooked in advance or even the night before. I find this dish reheats well in the microwave for convenience, but it is just as good served cold as a rice salad.

firecracker rice

long-grain white rice, measured to the
    400ml (14 fl oz) level in a measuring jug
    and cooked according to the method
    given on page 26 for Steamed Rice
2 tablespoons groundnut (peanut) oil
2 teaspoons sesame oil
3 tablespoons coarsely chopped garlic
1 finely chopped onion
2 tablespoons chilli bean sauce
salt and freshly ground black pepper, to taste
1 teaspoon chilli oil
3 tablespoons finely chopped spring
    onions
2 tablespoons finely chopped fresh
    coriander

P Can be prepared ahead: cover the rice and refrigerate for up to 24 hours. To reheat the finished dish, complete up to the end of stage 4, cool, cover and refrigerate for up to 24 hours. Reheat in a wok for 5–10 minutes, then complete the recipe.

1 Cook the rice at least 2 hours ahead or the night before. Allow it to cool thoroughly by spreading it on a baking sheet. When it is cool, cover and refrigerate. When it is completely cold, proceed with the rest of the recipe. **P**

2 Heat a wok over high heat. When it is hot, add the groundnut and sesame oils. When they are very hot and slightly smoking, add the garlic and onion and stir-fry for 2 minutes.

3 Add the rice and continue to stir-fry for 5 minutes.

4 Add the chilli bean sauce, salt, pepper and chilli oil, and continue to stir-fry for 3–4 minutes. **P**

5 Sprinkle in the spring onions and coriander, and continue to stir-fry for 1 further minute.

6 Turn onto a warm platter and serve hot, or leave to cool and serve cold as a rice salad.

Many years ago, this would have been a difficult recipe to make in the West as fresh coriander was hard to find. However, today it is available in abundance in supermarkets so everyone can sample this easy and delicious noodle dish. To make it completely vegetarian, use vegetarian stock.

stir-fried coriander and garlic noodles

175g (6 oz) thin or flat dried rice noodles

225g (8 oz) fresh or frozen peas

2 tablespoons groundnut (peanut) oil

2 teaspoons sesame oil

2 tablespoons coarsely chopped garlic

3 tablespoons home-made chicken or
  vegetarian stock (see pages 23–6)
  or quality store-bought fresh stock

salt and freshly ground black pepper, to taste

3 tablespoons finely chopped fresh
  coriander

6 tablespoons finely chopped spring
  onions

1 Soak the noodles in a large bowl of hot water. If using flat noodles, soak for 25 minutes; if using thin noodles, soak for 20 minutes. When soft, drain well in a colander and discard the water.

2 If you are using fresh peas, blanch them in boiling water for 2 minutes, drain and set aside. If you are using frozen peas, thaw at room temperature.

3 Heat a wok over high heat until it is hot, then add both the oils. When they are hot, add the garlic and stir-fry for 10 seconds.

4 Add the rice noodles and continue to stir-fry for 2 minutes.

5 Now add the stock, salt, pepper, peas, coriander and spring onions, and continue to stir-fry for 2 minutes.

6 Turn onto a warm platter and serve at once.

This is one of the quickest and easiest noodle dishes I know. Be sure to get the best oyster sauce you can find and the recipe will literally cook itself.

pork and oyster sauce noodles

225g (8 oz) flat dried rice noodles

2 teaspoons sesame oil

1 tablespoon light soy sauce

1 tablespoon groundnut (peanut) oil

450g (1 lb) minced pork

5 tablespoons oyster sauce

3 tablespoons home-made chicken stock (see page 23) or quality store-bought fresh stock

2 teaspoons sugar

1 tablespoon finely chopped fresh ginger

6 tablespoons finely chopped spring onions

1 Soak the rice noodles in a large bowl of hot water for 25 minutes. When soft, drain well in a colander, discarding the water. Toss with the sesame oil and soy sauce, and set aside.

2 Heat a wok over high heat until it is hot, then add the groundnut oil. When it is hot and slightly smoking, add the pork and stir-fry for 2 minutes, breaking up any clumps of meat.

3 Add the oyster sauce, stock and sugar, and stir-fry for 3 minutes.

4 Add the ginger, spring onions and the noodles, and stir-fry briskly for 4 minutes. Make sure the pork is thoroughly cooked and that there is no pink.

5 Turn onto a warm platter and serve at once.

These delicious noodles can either make a fast meal by themselves or a satisfying side dish. They are easy to make and even better to eat. The noodles can be cooked in advance and will keep for up to 24 hours, covered, in a refrigerator. To make the dish completely vegetarian, use vegetarian oyster sauce.

savoury garlic noodles

225g (8 oz) dried or fresh egg noodles
4 teaspoons sesame oil
1½ tablespoons groundnut (peanut) oil
5 tablespoons coarsely chopped garlic
1 tablespoon light soy sauce
3 tablespoons oyster sauce or vegetarian oyster sauce
3 tablespoons home-made chicken or vegetarian stock (see pages 23–6) or quality store-bought fresh stock
freshly ground black pepper, to taste
3 tablespoons finely chopped spring onions

1 Cook the noodles for 3–5 minutes in a large pan of boiling water. Immerse in cold water for 1 minute or until cool and drain thoroughly. Toss with half the sesame oil and set aside.

2 Heat a wok over high heat until it is hot, then add the groundnut oil. When it is hot, add the garlic and stir-fry for 30 seconds or until golden brown.

3 Add the cooked noodles and stir-fry briskly for 3 minutes, mixing well.

4 Finally, add the soy sauce, oyster or vegetarian oyster sauce, stock, pepper, spring onions and the remaining sesame oil, mixing well.

5 Turn onto a warm platter and serve at once.

desserts

This is a quick version of a Hong-Kong inspired recipe. Make sure you use a wok that is non-stick, because an ordinary carbon-steel wok will react with the acid from the berries or the coconut and turn the food greyish, which is unappetising. Prepare the recipe up to stage 4 in advance, if you like.

melon with coconut milk

2 x 400ml (14 fl oz) tins coconut milk
6 tablespoons sugar
150ml (5 fl oz) cold milk
1.5kg (3 lb) ripe honeydew melons
   (about 1 or 2)

GARNISH
handful fresh basil leaves

P Can be prepared ahead, in two stages if wished: complete to the end of stage 2, cover and refrigerate for up to 24 hours. Then prepare up to the end of stage 4, cover with cling film and refrigerate for up to 6 hours.

1 In a non-stick wok or large non-stick frying pan, combine the coconut milk and sugar, bring to simmering point and simmer for 10 minutes, or until the mixture begins to thicken.

2 Add the cold milk and remove from the heat. Allow to cool thoroughly. Pour into a bowl, cover with cling film and refrigerate. This can be prepared the night before. P

3 With a melon baller, scoop out balls from about a quarter of the melon. Place in a bowl, wrap with cling film and refrigerate.

4 Now peel and deseed the remaining melon. Cut into large pieces and purée in a blender or food processor until it is reduced to a thick liquid. Pour into a medium-sized bowl, cover with cling film and refrigerate. P

5 When you are ready to serve, combine the two mixtures as follows. Take a soup tureen and pour the coconut mixture into one side of it and the honeydew mixture on the other side, forming a yin/yang pattern. Add the melon balls, garnish with the basil leaves and give a few gentle stirs. Serve.

This is a sharp but refreshing finish to any meal, elegant and very easy to prepare. It requires no cooking and all the work can be done several hours in advance. Serve it after a family meal or a party for friends.

strawberries with candied ginger

450g (1 lb) fresh strawberries

3 tablespoons sugar

3 tablespoons crystallised ginger or
stem ginger in syrup

1 tablespoon orange liqueur

P Can be prepared ahead: cover and refrigerate for up to 4 hours.

1 Wipe the strawberries with a damp cloth and hull. Cut in half and toss gently with the sugar.

2 If using stem ginger, drain off the syrup. Finely chop the ginger and toss gently with the strawberries. Add the orange liqueur and toss again.

3 Cover with cling film and refrigerate for at least 1 hour before serving. P

I rarely serve sweet desserts at the end of a meal, preferring fruit instead for a refreshing finale, but this easy-to-make dessert provides a perfect finish. Like the strawberries with candied ginger (opposite), this does not require cooking and the oranges can be prepared well in advance.

orange salad

4 large oranges
handful shredded basil leaves

P Can be prepared ahead: cover and refrigerate for up to 8 hours.

1 Peel the oranges and with a small sharp knife, slice them horizontally into pieces 0.5cm (¼ in) thick. P

2 Arrange on a platter, garnish with the basil and serve.

I love this simple dessert, which is quickly made in a wok. Any combination of berries in season will do, and the more variety the better. I love it with cream or vanilla ice cream. Whether you use a wok or a pan, make sure it is non-stick, because the acid of the berries will react with carbon steel or iron.

summer berries with lemongrass

3 stalks fresh lemongrass
110g (4 oz) sugar
150ml (5 fl oz) water
175g (6 oz) strawberries
175g (6 oz) raspberries
175g (6 oz) blueberries

1 Peel the lemongrass stalks to the tender whitish centre and crush them with the flat of a knife. Then cut into 7.5cm (3 in) pieces.

2 Using a non-stick or coated wok, bring the sugar and water to the boil. Add the lemongrass, turn the heat to low, cover tightly and simmer for 10 minutes. Remove the lemongrass stalks and discard.

3 Add the berries and cook on a low heat for 2 minutes, just enough to warm them through. Remove from the heat and stir gently.

4 Turn onto a dish or individual bowls and serve at once.

This exotic-sounding dessert is really very simple to make. So simple, in fact, that my mother made it often just because it was so easy. The oranges are essential as they add a refreshing touch to this delicate custard, but it will also combine well with other fresh fruits. Serve it with your favourite biscuits.

steamed custard with lemon

4 whole eggs

2 egg yolks

8 tablespoons sugar

600ml (1 pint) whole milk

2 tablespoons lemon zest

1 orange, segmented

1 In a medium-sized bowl, combine the eggs and yolks with the sugar. Then add the milk and lemon zest, and mix well.

2 Next set up a steamer or put a rack into a wok and fill it with 5cm (2 in) water. Bring the water to the boil over a high heat. Pour the milk mixture into a heatproof shallow bowl and then carefully lower it into the steamer or onto the rack. Turn the heat down to low, cover the wok tightly and steam gently for 20 minutes.

3 Allow to cool slightly and gently drain off the excess liquid.

4 Serve while still warm, with the orange segments.

MENU PLANNING

HOW TO EAT CHINESE FOOD

Traditionally, Chinese meals always consist of a soup, a rice, noodle or bread dish, a vegetable dish and at least two other dishes, which may be mainly meat, fish or chicken. The meal may be preceded and concluded with tea, but during the meal itself, soup – really a broth – will be the only beverage. That is, soup is drunk, not as a first course as in the West, but throughout the meal.

The exception to this is at a banquet when soup, if it is served at all, comes at the end of the meal or as a palate-cleanser at several points during the dinner. On such occasions, wine, spirits, beer or even fruit juice will be drunk with the food. At banquets (which are really elaborate dinner parties), dishes are served one at a time so that the individual qualities of each dish can be properly savoured. There may be as many as eight to twelve courses. Rice will not be served except at the end of the meal when fried rice might be offered to anyone who has any appetite left.

At ordinary family meals all the dishes comprising the meal are served together, including the soup. The food is placed in the centre of the table. Each person has their own rice bowl into which they put a generous amount of steamed rice. Then, using their chopsticks, they help themselves to a little of one dish, transferring this to their rice bowl. Once they have eaten this, together with some rice, they will have a chopstick-full of another dish. No Chinese would dream of heaping their rice bowl with what they regarded as their full share of any dish before proceeding to eat. Eating is a communal affair and each diner will take care to see that everyone else at the table receives a fair share of everything. You can see what a civilising and socialising practice this is.

Of course, you can eat Chinese food any way you like. I think it blends deliciously with many European dishes. If you are new to Chinese cooking, you may find it easier to familiarise yourself with the cuisine by trying out just one or two dishes at a time and incorporating them into a non-Chinese menu. Chinese soups, for example, make excellent starters and stir-fried vegetables are delicious with grills and roasts.

When you do devise an all-Chinese meal, try to see that you have a good mix of textures, flavours, colours and shapes. Apart from a staple dish, such as steamed rice, you should opt for a variety of meat, poultry and fish. It is better to serve one meat and one fish dish rather than two meat dishes, even if the meats are different. It will also be a better-balanced meal (and easier to prepare) if you use a variety of cooking methods. Serve a stir-fried dish with a braised, steamed or cold dish. It's important to try to select one or two things that can be prepared in advance. Avoid doing more than two stir-fried dishes as you will thus avoid frantic activity at the last minute.

Chinese cooking can be very time-consuming. The recipes are based on the expectation that you will cook two meat, chicken or fish dishes per meal. (This is in addition to a vegetable dish, rice or noodles and, perhaps, a soup.) This way the total meat, chicken or fish allowance per person will be about 175–225g (6–8 oz). If you prefer to cook just one such dish, then you will probably have to double the quantities given in the recipe. This does at least mean that you will have a chance to try the authentic taste of Chinese food without quite so much work. Once you gain confidence, you will be able to cope with preparing more dishes and can serve a more authentic Chinese meal.

SUGGESTED MENUS FOR ENTERTAINING SIMPLY BUT ELEGANTLY

Twenty years ago when I was much younger and more naive (I am a lot older now but no wiser), I entertained extravagantly. My dinner parties would have a minimum of twelve guests and never less than twelve courses. I would spend days preparing elaborate and obscure Chinese dishes. I had much more time then and I took great pleasure and enjoyment in preparing those meals.

However, now that I have a heavy travel schedule with all the pressures of a modern busy life, my style of entertaining has changed radically. Now when I entertain, I usually have no more than six guests and just three courses. I discovered that my friends enjoyed those intimate dinners just as much as my lavish spreads of the past.

Here then is how I entertain today, simply but still elegantly. I have also included menus for quick everyday meals.

When entertaining, keep the following tips in mind:

- Invite friends you really want to see. Spending three or four hours at the dinner table with good friends is my idea of bliss. Remember that the conversation and the mix of people is almost as important as the food and wine. Don't invite the same guests all the time; it is nice to mix and match your friends. Never have a party where all the guests are from the same profession; nothing is worse than talking shop all evening.
- Don't skimp; buy the best ingredients and choose good wines. This is vital, especially if you have only three courses. Also your chances of success are greater if your dishes are memorable.
- Don't attempt new dishes; always entertain with tried and true recipes or dishes that you feel comfortable with. You don't need the additional stress of wondering whether the dish will be any good or not. However, you should feel free to combine dishes from different cuisines. For example, you could begin with a soup (made ahead of time), followed by a lovely stir-fried chicken dish with rice, and finally a stir-fried vegetable dish.
- Avoid trying to impress your guests. I always think it is grander to make delicious, quick, simple food than to present pretentious mediocre dishes. There is no need to stick rigidly to other people's rules about food; if you like fish with red wine, then serve them together.

- Remember to cook dishes that are within the scope of home cooks. Chefs apart, I don't think your guests should expect you to be proficient in restaurant cooking. When you are planning a meal, don't include more than two stir-fry dishes. There are many recipes in this book that can be prepared ahead of time.
- Light meals are usually the best-remembered ones. That means light or no sauces; no red meat; stick to fish or chicken. Nothing is worse than a heavy meal that can stay with you for the whole night.
- Soups, especially good ones, are an elegant opening. I like them because I can make them days, even a week, ahead. They freeze extremely well and reheat beautifully.
- Think about your dinner for a few moments before you plan it. All too often, home cooks plunge into organising a dinner party without thought to the balance of the meal, logistics, etc. Think about how you would feel as a guest at this dinner. If your instincts tell you that the dinner will be good, the chances are it will be.
- Begin the evening with champagne. Bubbles are always a festive start to any meal and they immediately put everyone in a good mood. This is an important factor, which will determine how the rest of the evening flows.
- Finally, never panic. If something doesn't turn out the way you thought it should, don't mention it to your guests. Just patch it up as best as you can, smile, have another glass of champagne and enjoy yourself.

Remember that the following menus are merely suggestions. Feel free to mix and match your favourite dishes to create your own Quick Wok Menus.

QUICK ENTERTAINING
CURRIED CASHEW NUTS (page 40)
DELECTABLE CHICKEN LIVERS (page 38)
SESAME SEED CHICKEN (page 34)

A QUICK WINTER WOK TREAT
VEGETARIAN EGGFLOWER SOUP (page 48)
BRAISED BEEF WITH BEANCURD (page 106)
STIR-FRIED SPINACH WITH GINGER (page 122)

ELEGANT AND FAST DINNER PARTY
SALT AND PEPPER PRAWNS (page 28)
TOMATO EGGFLOWER SOUP
WITH BEANCURD (page 50)
STEAMED GINGER FISH (page 68)
ORANGE SALAD (page 151)

POPULAR QUICK NOODLE MEAL
PORK AND OYSTER SAUCE NOODLES (page 144)
STIR-FRIED BEANS WITH
CHILLI BEANCURD (page 118)

COMFORT WOK MEAL
VIETNAMESE PHO SOUP (page 53)
FIVE-SPICE CHIPS (page 124)
STIR-FRIED GREEN BEANS
WITH GARLIC (page 130)

FAST FOOD FOR SEAFOOD LOVERS
MUSSELS WITH GINGER AND
SPRING ONIONS (page 56)
GARLIC PRAWNS (page 58)
SPICY TUNA (page 74)

FAST VEGETARIAN WOK FEAST
COLD AUBERGINE SALAD (page 111)
CURRIED COURGETTES (page 119)
STIR-FRIED SPINACH WITH GINGER (page 122)
STIR-FRIED VEGETARIAN PHAD THAI (page 139)

EASY WOK MENU FOR SUMMER
STEAMED SCALLOPS WITH
BLACK BEANS (page 62)
CHICKEN IN LETTUCE CUPS (page 83)
MIC'S AUBERGINE PURÉE (page 112)

INDEX

Note: Page numbers in **bold** refer to major text sections. Vegetarian recipes are in *italic*.